An Endorphin Release, Now Please!

An Expose Of The Sandwich Generation

Hasmik Rakijian

ISBN: 1974314316
ISBN: 13- 9781974314317

DEDICATION

To my husband, daughter and son, my mother and father,
my mother-in-law and father-in-law, my husband's aunt and uncle,
I love you all.

TABLE OF CONTENTS

ACKNOWLEDGMENTS

First, I want to acknowledge and thank T. Harv Eker, the author of <u>Secrets of the Millionaire Mind</u>, and the organization he has built teaching courage to take action to follow your passion. Peak Potentials Training Inc., based in Canada, was instrumental in the launch of my first book, But She's Not A Guy, and my continued follow through as an author and speaker with now my third book. The two training sessions I attended, first: "The Millionaire Mind Training" was eye opening and filled with moments of self-realization and renewal. The second training "Train the Trainer" was captivating, very freeing and self-actualizing. I have my broken warrior arrow and picture to prove the transformation I accomplished! The greatest way to overcome fear is to take that initial first step. The next steps will reveal themselves and the path will be easier to follow! So go for it!

My second acknowledgment goes to Gerry Rose of Integrity, Arizona, a person who seems to interject into my life from time to time, in seemingly the right season of change and the right reason of influence. He is a long-time, perhaps over 20 years, acquaintance whom I met through a networking session at the Carlsbad Chamber of Commerce. He has given me nuggets of wisdom to pursue my dreams in a timely fashion. He encouraged me, rather than to seek perfection as the highest importance, to instead focus on timely completion. He made me understand that seeking perfection is honorable but unattainable and can lead to paralysis and procrastination. Completing the work to the best of your ability in a given time allows you the freedom to do more and complete more fine works. Thank you Gerry for lifting obstacles so I can go forward.

Third, I want to thank and acknowledge Chris Majer, the author of <u>The Power to Transform</u>. Interestingly, I applied for employment to Chris' organization, The Human Potential Project, and wrote him a follow up memo on his philosophies of organizational development. To my surprise, he personally responded. I promised I would read his book and follow up with him again. I challenge myself to learn something new from each of life's experiences. I incorporated into my life the teachings in Majer's book about how our choices are what lead to our current and future situations. Looking back, it is easy to blame other people and external circumstances for misfortunes, but the truth is we all have choices and being accountable for our life and our future is true empowerment. Seeking credible information from reliable sources to determine your options is critical to make the right choices. I also learned as we get older or have credentials to our name, not to think we have experienced or know it all. It is acceptable to give yourself permission to be a "beginner" at any age, and remain open to learning and growing!

Chapter One

How about some R&R?

R&R used to mean rest and relaxation (R&R1). For members of the sandwich generation in this twenty-first century, R&R means relationships and responsibilities (R&R2)! We have more than our fair share of R&R2 and we need much more of R&R1! Just take a snapshot of time and see what a sandwich generation member has to endure:

My daughter, who is attending University of California Santa Barbara, just called saying her bike was stolen and she needs money for a new bike, textbooks, and her first month rent for her sophomore year in college. My son, who is in eighth grade, says he needs help with his homework and that he feels congested and needs to use his inhaler. My husband is at work and needs to stay late to finish his research project and may have to pull an all nighter. I have a breakfast seminar that I am hosting tomorrow morning on planning for long-term care, as I have my own financial planning practice. My ninety years old aunt calls and says the lights went out in her block and the house burglar alarm is sounding and she can't figure out how to deactivate or "silence the damn thing." My 86 year-old widowed mother-in-law, who now lives with us due to macular degeneration and symptoms of depression such as not eating or bathing, is wondering what we are having for dinner. My mother calls and says that my 80 year old father's blood pressure just fell and he passed out on the toilet, and she has just called 911 and she, age 70, has excruciating back pain from helping break his fall. She needs a ride to the hospital emergency because she doesn't want go alone. All this happened in just one night!

Welcome to the life of a hard-core member of the sandwich generation. I have started a regimen of herbs, particularly to help with menopausal hot flashes and mood swings. I am trying these new hypnotherapy CD's on finding your peace in your imaginary peaceful place. Every time I try to find quiet time to listen to them, someone interrupts and snatches me out of my peaceful place and back into my hectic reality. I am seeing a therapist who tells me to set parameters in my interactions and shields to protect myself and my sanity. I have a personal trainer to help me stay in shape and fight off stress by having endorphins released to fight the free radicals in my body. I do all this and more to stay focused so I can run my business and life. I also try to get intermittent pampering such as pedicures, manicures, facials or massages, as my meager pampering budget allows. I have several books from various Christian preachers on peace and happiness along with the Holy Book, the Bible, which I read every evening prior to bed. I pray several times a day, and I have committed and recommitted all my cares to God for Him to handle. I am willing to try anything to maintain my sanity and not have a nervous breakdown or spiral into a depression.

It is increasingly hard to focus on work and clients when so many personal demands are placed on me daily. Prioritization of life's current events takes precedence. Relationships become paramount. My time and life is so valuable that I cannot waste it on relationships that do not add to my well being in some fashion, whether social, cultural, educational, spiritual or financial. Between email, voice mail, cell phone, business phone, junk mail and snail mail, it's no wonder we are overwhelmed and bombarded with demands for our time, energy and money. We have three timeshare weeks that we are adamant on using each year, but the complexity of our lives and schedules makes it increasingly hard to coordinate the time off for family vacations. So we squeeze in three day weekend getaways here and there, again to maintain our sanity and so that we don't lose touch with each other in the mire of life. I keep reminding myself, "This is the day that the Lord has made, so rejoice in it!" So I try to focus on Jesus and stay steady and faithful through the storms of life. I keep reminding myself, "This too shall pass." It just isn't passing fast enough. Patience is also paramount.

It's a peculiar predicament! You raise your children and you expect that once they have grown that you and your husband will enjoy independence to some degree to travel and do those things that you could not do while the children were infants. No one mentioned that all of a sudden you have adult dependents such as your parents and your spouse's parents and other elders, as is in my case, such as aunts and uncles that did not have children. As good children, nieces and nephews with fine Christian upbringing you assist them with their needs as they age and become frail. There are just too many affairs to attend to when in many cases you have not fully attended to your own concerns such as your own business, your child's school events, medical and dental appointments, and important matters such as retirement and estate planning.

With a child in college and having my own business, retirement savings seem to be a low priority. Thank God I had worked twelve years for a Fortune 500 technology company and am vested in my prior employers defined benefit pension plan that will provide some monthly income once I reach age 55. My husband and I have been fairly frugal and the Lord has been gracious to us in that we now own three single-family homes. One is our primary residence, and the other two are rentals. Two are California coastal real estate and the other an inland property where there's promise of future growth. We hope to transfer these to our children as their inheritance.

Life just takes on a whole new level of meaning and nuance when you have to assist your aging father, because he feels discomfort from the catheter, and he's not lying in a comfortable position in what will probably be his death bed. It's simply disconcerting to know that someone is dying, and you have to continue on with your life poised and smiling and servicing others. You also can't discuss your emotions too much with others because everyone has their own issues and matters. To discuss it briefly is OK, but prolonged or frequent discussions may cause people to walk away if they see you coming.

You cannot let these matters of family illness and deaths affect your work. I ask myself often how on earth does our country's President put his head to the pillow at night and actually fall asleep. Then he has to wake up and go through his day in complete control while in the public eye regardless of what is going on around the world or in his own personal life. The United States President literally has the weight of the United States and the world on his shoulders. I feel for the first lady as to how much moral support could one give when the world's critical eye is on your husband, his work and your family. I also ponder about how Christ took on the burdens and sins of the world, was persecuted and ridiculed as he hung on the cross for our salvation. He did this to provide us with eternal salvation in heaven, plus comfort, peace, joy, and abundance here during our earthly stay. Christ's death and resurrection gave us the kind of peace that surpasses human understanding because it sparks from our faith in Jesus Christ.

My husband and I have been working diligently to achieve not only meeting today's needs for ourselves and our children, but also to meet our needs as we age and to leave something of significance behind for our children and future grandchildren and our church and then potentially other charities. We strongly believe that we want to achieve our higher purpose by using our God given talents to glorify Him by fulfilling our passion and our mission on earth. In terms of that mission of passion, it is continually evolving. We both feel that we are being pruned and trained for this higher purpose. We both have gone through various trials and tribulations, and as we progress through each storm, we come to a rainbow. Then as soon as we start enjoying that rainbow and the clarity and peace, another storm of life's endless drama approaches. I have learned that storms cannot be avoided. You just have to hunker down and persist through them and "walk by faith not by sight" through each coming storm. People ask me how is it that you can keep smiling through all that is happening around you and with you. It is my faith in Christ, and that peace beyond understanding, and knowing that he has my back and all this swirling in life is coming to a greater good in my life. Knowing that all is not happening "to" me, but rather happening "for" me is a reassuring thought. So I smile through it, because I know God is prepping me for something bigger and better!

The late and great Reverend Martin Luther King said in his last speech prior to his assassination "I have been to the mountain top…I don't fear anything or any man, for my eyes have seen the coming of the Lord!" His eloquent and hopeful speech truly embraces that in his lifetime walk with the Lord, he was at the base of the mountain or the valley and one careful step at a time he climbed up that mountain of life's storms. As he climbed, he knew that the Lord was uplifting him until he reached the top of the mountain where he was doing the Lord's work in complete connection with the Almighty. Martin Luther King knew and loved God! From his words "Nothing really matters now," I sense that Reverend King knew that his hour of death was near, like Jesus knew at the Garden of Gethsemane that his time was coming and that Judas would soon betray him. As a mortal man, Reverend King was afraid, but as a brother in Christ he had no fear as he knew he was entering the true promise land and he was soon to be in the Glory of God's presence in heaven. Alleluia!

I have never physically climbed up a steep mountain, but I have seen those who have on television. You have to carefully plan each footing lest you fall. Other than that, climbing a mountain is a leap of faith and an act of courage. So as we go through trials and tribulations, as we address all the minute and major demands of our various relationships, we are serving a higher power. Our foot may slip at times, as we are human. Yet, the Lord will provide the guidance to lead our path if we let him. I have to continuously remind myself that I am doing all this not to serve man only, but as an act of service for God's glory. I am climbing this mountain of life, step by step, enduring the pain and frustration while carrying my cross to the top. I know that as I take the steps necessary and upon arrival at the top of the mountain, in full commitment to the Lord, I experience the exhilaration of abundant joy, and that peace that surpasses all understanding. God will have a place for me in his heavenly mansion as the Holy Bible promises salvation to those who have faith in Christ.

At age 48, this week I understood that God loves me regardless of what I do or don't do. In other words, we do not have to *earn* God's love. God's love is unconditional; it's free by his grace. He sent His only son to die for us on the cross so that our sins would be forgiven and erased and so that we could have eternal life with Him. He did this not because we asked Him or because we earned or deserved it. He did it out of love, with His infinite mercy and His abundant grace.

I knew about God's unconditional love and that through faith in Jesus we are saved and lead to receive the gifts of the Holy Spirit that manifest by doing good towards others. But I was putting undue pressure on myself that I had to do good to stay in God's favor. I didn't understand God's unconditional love. I felt that I had to meet everyone's needs including my children's, my husband's, my parents', my in-laws', and my clients' to be considered good enough to be counted as one of God's children. Well, I suddenly realized or had a revelation that God doesn't expect me to be Jesus. I am not perfect like Jesus, nor will I ever be. I can only do well by others as much as humanely possible without driving myself crazy or sick. It takes faith, in the size of a little mustard seed, that translates to love and hope in our lives and to all those that our life touches. We can only bear the cross that we can bear, and God said He wouldn't give us more than we can bear. Knowing something, and understanding it enough so as to apply it to your everyday life situations, are two different things. That is why I continue to study the Word of God everyday for such revelations of understanding or as they are termed "pearls of wisdom".

In the following chapters, I want to introduce you to my many relationships and the myriad situations that I have encountered. I will share with you the elders in my life and their various circumstances and how we have addressed their needs. I'll also write about my children's adventure to find their passion and purpose. I will also share my husband's and my pursuit of seizing some nuggets of time alone to just be together or possibly talk about our goals. I hope that reading this book will serve as a fishbowl and an inspirational guide to all who are in…no not the "Twilight Zone", although it may sometimes feel like it; rather, in the "Sandwich Generation".

Half My Life

For half my life
I've lived and loved.
I've learned and traveled,
And been spiritually fed.

For half my life
I've planned and worked
Then worked some more
And planned some more.

For half my life
I've danced and sang
And laughed and cried
And waited on the Lord.

For half my life
I've saved and spent
I've bought and sold
Then gave away the old.

For half my life
Is gone away
In a flicker of time
That I can't regain

Now at midlife,
Who is to say,
How the other half
Of my life will play?

Chapter Two

Is There A Puppy In The House?

It was in the beginning of the New Year, that my husband and I decided, together, that his mother should come live with us. One year later, we laugh, roll our eyes and pass the blame for the decision to each other, in jest, because it hasn't been easy and rather uncomfortable. After 24 years of marriage, it is difficult to bring a parent into our home and walk the fine line of independence versus disrespect. For example, when you are used to coming and going as you please, now there is an underlying pressure to notify where you are going and what time is your expected return. During the week we often don't cook a complete meal or sit down for dinner, maybe opting for just a quick sandwich or salad, whereas she's waiting to have a sit down family meal. I like to putter in my kitchen alone in peace in the early morning while the coffee is brewing. Now she's awake even before me, and is sitting in her favorite chair to which she has proclaimed exclusive sitting-rights waiting to have breakfast and conversation together. Her favorite seat happens to be my husband's leather chair that is in prime position in front of his big screen TV that the children and I gave him for his 50th birthday. Now my husband insists that I speak to her about the chair! "But, she's your mother!" I retort.

We moved her with us out of concern for her health and safety. It was becoming more and more evident to my husband that she was losing weight due to not eating and that she had become increasingly lonely. After her husband's passing, she still had a social circle that included her sister-in-law, a couple of her neighbors, but as each of them aged, died or moved closer to their children, she became lonelier. My husband would go once a week to take her grocery shopping. It was more of an obstacle course for my husband as she insists on going from one store to the other for specific "sale" items or "choicer" selection. He helps her get in and out of the car, and suffers through the cash payment process with the counting of the coins, and grumbles as she only buys in small quantities ensuring his weekly visits. Her other son would come and take her to church each Sunday as he was in the church choir.

Her eating disorder came into light when we had dressy occasions or happy family gatherings, like New Years Eve Gala, her son's 50th birthday celebration, and my daughter's black-tie Debutante Ball. In all three occasions, she had not eaten all day and in her excitement in the evening she ate perhaps too much for her shrinking stomach, had a vasovagl response and turned pale, vomited and passed out. On the first occasion, we had to call 911. The other occasions we recognized the symptoms and revived her with water and ice and laying her down.

Her eyesight was starting to weaken due to macular degeneration. Part of her not eating could also be that she didn't trust herself to cook or it was getting more difficult to prepare a meal. Her eyesight is too weak to read. Her TV was too small to see, so she called the cable company and cut her cable because she didn't want to pay for it if she couldn't see it. My husband one day came over and she's just sitting there on the couch, alone, doing nothing. Also, some time ago, she had tripped and fallen on an exposed tree root in the street that had cracked through the sidewalk cement. She now has a cane to support her weight due to a slight limp that materialized after her bone fusion surgery. She is too vain to use the cane, or to wear orthopedic support shoes with elevated soles, that she should be wearing. So given these circumstances, we felt it would be better it she came and lived with us.

My husband's brother and his wife have their own circumstances to deal with. My sister-in-law is an only child and has her aging parents who come to the United States each year and stay with her for about six months and then return home to Istanbul, Turkey. This last time, however, her mother, who has been trying to control her blood pressure, ended up with surgery on a blocked artery and is in recovery. Her mother also needs another surgery to unblock the other artery in the near future. My brother-in-law also had encephalitis at one time after having gone to a Caribbean island vacation, and undergoing a long rehabilitation, so we were concerned about adding undue pressure on him, so my husband and I took on the responsibility for his mother's wellbeing.

In our Armenian traditional culture, we care for our elderly. Both my husband and I had a grandmother living at home with us when we were in our early teens. There is a slight difference, however, in that the grandmothers were our maternal grandmothers not our fathers' mother. Traditionally, the wife living with her mother seems to work out more comfortably that the wife living with her mother-in-law. The key factor in the relationship is how the husband or son relates to each, and whether the husband and wife bond is solidly maintained. The Good Book says, "A man shall leave his parents and cleave to his wife". So, as long as everyone understands who is cleaving to whom, the order of things can remain peaceful. If that order is not maintained, then there can be chaos in the home.

There is another important factor and that is the personality, attitude, nature or spirit of the people involved. My family and home is happy. Praise God! We sing, dance, laugh, and tell jokes. Our dinners together, which are usually on the weekends, are truly an event. My husband is the primary instigator of our jovial escapades, followed by my son and daughter, all talented, all full of life. We often joke that we should have a camera in the house for a web-based reality show that people can tune into. My husband and two children are all impersonators, comedians and singers. They can do people's voices and mannerisms and often they know scenes from sitcoms that they can reenact verbatim. My husband can take any real life situation and find the humor in it. He really lightens my world with his humorous viewpoints and storytelling and even our children start laughing so much to the point of tears like they just inhaled a tank of laughing gas.

My mother-in-law, however, just doesn't get it or doesn't want to get it. She sits there with straight face and somber mood like a damper on life. She creates a depressing aura. I try to explain to her even though I don't always get into it with the three of them, I just enjoy the spirit and the immense joy that they have together. She, on the other hand, just doesn't get it. Maybe her life or family relationship wasn't this way. In my childhood, my father was always the center of love, humor and optimism in my family. These endearing qualities are what I admired in my husband, but he inherited them from his father's side, not his mother. Yet she is his mother and she needs us. So, out of respect, we just endure it and we also try hard to ignore it and not create a damper on our family.

Often I think that she has a deep-rooted selfish streak, or maybe a feeling of inadequacy. A sort of sulkiness that says I will not enjoy this because it's not about me or for me, like she wants to rain on your parade. She displays this subtle and continuous gnawing pessimism that seems to be the undertone of her life. She speaks about prayer and how the Good Lord answers her prayers, but doesn't know how to apply or accept joy, peace and happiness in her life. She is either expecting from others, or pretentiously worrying about somebody or a situation, as though she is doing something constructive by worrying and then telling us how worried she was.

As an example, if we tell my mother that my husband and I are going out to dinner together, she is genuinely happy for us and wants us to have a good time. She understands how hard we work and often don't see each other or have quality time together, so she's happy that we are making time for each other. My mother-in-law is just the opposite. We are almost afraid to tell her that we plan to go out, because in her thinking she wonders why she's not going with us, and thinks that others are going and we are excluding her. We know this by the questions she asks such as "Is my sister's mother-in-law going along?" She makes investigational phone calls to see if my mother or aunt is still home after we leave. It's a little pathetic and wearing on my nerves. Then she makes us feel guilty by staying up and sitting in the dark on the couch until we get home. Rather creepy! It's comparable to a little child who feels excluded when mom and dad have to go out to an event where children are not invited or on a mommy and daddy only date-night.

Basically, like with children, we explained to her that if it's appropriate to take her or if she is invited then we'll go together, but otherwise we have our own life and we need to attend to our own agendas. So she sulks, she doesn't pick up the phone and invite her sister-in-law who has no one other than us in the world to extend herself out and make someone else happy, she just sits and sulks, expects and wants. We can only do what we can and not more, because we have our own lives, children, work, and other relationships to attend to. She cannot be the center of attention and we took her into our home and my feeling at this point is that we are doing more than enough. I feel that she is being ungrateful, selfish and expecting us to entertain her and meet her needs only. Unfortunately, we cannot drain ourselves to that extent especially to one who cannot be satisfied.

We finally cleared the air about where people sit and whose chair is whose, I did it very gently explaining that especially on the weekends when her son is home that he likes to sit on his leather chair and watch football on his big screen. My children know that's daddy's chair that he well deserved for his 50th birthday and would like to continue to enjoy. When he's not home, she's welcome to sit in it. Now, it has become almost an inside joke that as soon as my husband has left the chair my mother-in-law moves to it. When he comes in the room, she moves out of it. Rather uncomfortable, but it's her son and they know each other. So whatever seems uncomfortable to me, is not necessarily so for them.

The next thing we all noticed was that she smelled. Even my husband's chair started to smell. Her room smelled. Her bathroom smelled and it was seeping into the living room area as her bedroom is on the first floor. Men do not approach these things very gingerly, so my husband said to her very callously "Mom, you smell, you need to take showers more often." The problem is she doesn't smell it. My children and I smelled it, but she did not. I told her that her son loves her and that he wouldn't say she smelled if she did not. Why would he tell her that otherwise? She thinks he's saying it to just annoy her. I told her that since she just took a shower, there is no smell now. I told her as soon as I smell the odor; I will let her know so we can figure it out.

One day she came out of her room with that smell. It turned out that it was some old cologne from Turkey that she had for over 10 years, in fact it was her husband's and she was using it. I told her it was old and it did not smell good on her that she really should stop using it. She stopped using it but it did not help. The same odor came back. I asked her if she uses deodorant. She said she doesn't sweat so she doesn't use deodorant. I said everybody sweats! She asked me sarcastically if I use deodorant every day. I said yes after I shower, I put on deodorant before I get dressed everyday or else I would smell also. So she started using deodorant. That helped, but it didn't take care of the smell.

I noticed that she doesn't drink any water. I told her that people who take medications usually drink plenty of water. Now I'm thinking it's the medications she's taking. I asked her if she had talked to her doctor about the medicines she's taking; maybe some are causing a strong scent. She said that our 90-year-old aunt, her sister-in-law, takes the same blood pressure pills and doesn't have an issue. Her sister-in-law hadn't mentioned that she smelled or anything. Well, when she goes over to her house she usually takes a shower before going there.

I was emptying the trash receptacles around the house because tomorrow was garbage day. She saw that I had emptied her receptacle and she said I'll take mine out myself. She wanted to take her own garbage bag from her bathroom into the garage to put into the large garbage can. Now, I'm curious. Usually, she sits and wants to be served. This was out of character. One day, I snuck in and looked under her sink and there was a box of depends under the sink. Now I understood why she doesn't drink water and why she never has to go to the bathroom as she says so proudly.

As she was helping me wrap to put away the breakable ornaments from the Christmas tree, it happened. I looked to hand her an ornament and all of a sudden she was gone. Left behind on my kitchen floor tile and on my hardwood floors in the hall, was a trail like an untrained puppy would leave. I got paper towels and wiped the trail before she came out to save her from embarrassment, and before my husband sees it and an unpleasant scene develops. She came out of her bathroom, with the exact scent that we have been discussing, the scent of urine. Since her eyes don't see well, I don't think she saw or knew that she had left the trail. I gathered that her dress and slip also had taken on some of the mishap. I gingerly said to her, "I'm going to do some laundry and did she have anything she wanted me to toss into the load?" She gave me a bag of her underwear. Then I said, "You know you wore that same dress yesterday. Why don't I wash that as well, while I'm doing this load?" She said OK, went and changed and gave me her slip and dress.

Basically, she has a bladder control problem as many women do, and she's too proud to admit it. She uses Depends. I'm not sure if she wears them regularly to protect from mishaps or maybe she runs out of them. She doesn't drink water, because she's afraid of increased flow. However, the inverse is that because she doesn't drink enough water, her urine intensifies and smells even more. More frequent showers and the deodorant are certainly helping! I asked our ninety-year old aunt, her sister-in-law, to help. Anne said her own olfactory sense doesn't work too well anymore. In other words, she doesn't have a strong sense of smell. She said that she advises her to wear protection, but she said she only uses it when she goes out on a special occasion. She also said she doesn't change very often. Perhaps she's concerned about the cost. We all know she's frugally frugal. Hard to maintain discreetness!

Chapter Three

Much Ado about Eggplant

Out of the kindness of his heart, my sister's husband, decided to pick up some items from the Armenian grocer that is near his place of work. He was thinking of my mother-in-law as I had told him in passing that she liked black olives, not the kalamata but the dry wrinkled ones, which our local Middle Eastern Store didn't carry often enough. She also liked the thin Japanese eggplant that you rarely find at the grocery store or if you find it it's priced like gold. So out of the kindness of his heart, he stopped by after work to bring these items to her.

Armenian dishes take extensive preparation, and I thought that we could make stuffed eggplant dolma with the meat and bulgur stuffing that I love. I thought that coring out the eggplant would be something that my mother-in-law could do while she's sitting at the table, and I would mix up the stuffing and stuff the eggplant. When I told her that he had brought the eggplant for her and I was thinking of doing the stuffed eggplant, she kind of grimaced. Like all of a sudden coring eggplant was too much work. My husband chimed in; because he doesn't like stuffed eggplant and would rather have it fried in olive oil, confirming that coring eggplant is hard work.

I had called my mother earlier, asked her for the recipe for the stuffed eggplant dolma, and if she had any of the appropriate coarseness of bulgur. She said she had some and would drop some by. At this moment, my mother comes in with the bulgur and also agrees that coring the dolma is too much work. By the way, my brother-in-law had bought the eggplant so that my mother-in-law would make her signature eman-bayeldi dish. My mother in law was raised in Istanbul, Turkey and this dish takes eggplant, green pepper, onions, and tomatoes and garlic all individually fried and placed neatly in a casserole and then baked. I make the more health conscious version of grilled or broiled vegetables, but the true taste is in the frying and blending of the flavors in the generous olive oil. When my mom said that, my mother in law wasn't jumping up and down to make that either. You see she is 87 years old and has decided for herself that she no longer can do or will even try to do those dishes. She would rather sit.

It took me a long time, about a year of living with her to understand this and to come to peace with it. She would rather sit. I had many discussions with her about "Mom, why don't you get up and walk around the garden or sit in the front of the house where you can watch the goings on, the neighbor's children playing, or the ocean view off in the distance. She did it when I mentioned it for that day and that moment, but then comes back and sits. She also sits in the same spot all the time. I even said, "Why don't you change around a bit, so you get a different view of the room? But she has her spot. She can sit there for hours, if I don't give her an assignment or a project. She folds my laundry, if I have too much, like when my daughter comes home from college with her trunk full of things to be laundered. She will occasionally get up to make a salad. She does have a daily chore of putting the dishes away from the dishwasher. She can't put the dirty ones in the dishwasher because she doesn't understand the concept of proper placement so that the water can move between the plates or so that they don't break. I found this out from experience after a couple of glasses broke and the dishes still came out dirty. So she only does the putting away. As I said, she prefers to sit.

My husband's 90 years old aunt is not like that. She will get up and find something to do. If she is over our house, she will offer to help set the table or clear the table after dinner. She'll bake a desert or make a side dish when she comes over. She'll laugh when we laugh, or talk about various things or ask how things are. I think it is all in the mind and the background. My mother-in-law is from the old country. Our aunt is Armenian but was second generation born in the United States in 1917. Her grandparents had come from the old country before the Genocide of the Armenians conducted by the Turkish Ottoman Empire in 1915.

In comparison, my mother-in-law just chooses to sit, not talk, and not laugh. I even advised her that if she sits all the time, she's likely to lose the muscles that she needs. She uses a cane as she had fallen about fifteen years ago on a tree trunk that was protruding from the city sidewalk near her house. She did have surgery as she had broken a thighbone and they used a pin to fuse the two bones together. She is Ok. She wobbles a bit because one leg is about half an inch shorter, but thank goodness she can walk with her cane for balance.

Fifteen years ago her doctor had measured her and advised her that she needs to get specialty shoes with a lift added by a cobbler. She wouldn't get them for two reasons. First reason was vanity. In her mind she thought it wouldn't be glamorous, as the shoes that she needs to wear are wide healed ones not narrow heals. Second reason was frugality. Since the insurance wouldn't pay for it and she had to buy the shoes and pay for the cobbler to add the additional thicker sole, she decided she was not going to spend the forty dollars. Now, she wobbles more and her back is now hurting her, and she even fell a few times as her balance is getting weaker as her muscles are getting weaker. I told her that we are going to get her more stable shoes with a lift and there's no two ways about it. I also advised her that instead of the $40 that she would have paid fifteen years ago, that she should be ready to spend at least a $100. We were lucky and she was happy that we found shoes she liked on sale for $60 and the cobbler charged $15, so she only spent $75. Her day was made because she saved those dollars. She said had I known that it was this comfortable with less back stress, I would have bought the shoes with the lift sooner.

Then her doctor's bill came, where now she had a Medicare deductible to pay for the doctor's visit that we took. The Medicare deductible was about $120. That ruined that day. She had the 90 years old aunt call to verify if she had to pay it. She asked me to call and I obliged and confirmed that she had to pay it. She still didn't like the answer. So she calls her older son, to check out the situation. He calls back and says yes you have to pay it. Then I need to write the check because her eyes don't see well enough to write the check, and she signs the check with crooked hand writing rather askew from the signature line, but it's good enough for an eighty-seven year old. So she continues to sit.

Truly, I have given up. I decided I couldn't be her entertainment. I am not the only one responsible for her. She has two sons that she needs to call and talk to if she wants something. I also told her that she has friends and other relatives that she could occasionally think of them and give them a call to see how they are rather than sitting and waiting for them to call her.

Back to the eggplant, I decided I would just make whatever I want to make, the way I want to make it following my mother's recipe. Now she gets up and butts in. "Isn't that too much meat for those eggplants?" she said. I just said "no". I didn't want to get into a discussion again about the meat, the eggplant or anything else for that matter. I had to thaw some ground beef and being frozen I couldn't just thaw half the package, so I will use it all. In her miserly thinking, she would refreeze the meat that was already once thawed. She would also only use half the can of tomato sauce and refrigerate the rest until it gets moldy and then we throw it away. Anyway, I pulled out some green pepper and tomatoes and stuffed them as well with the extra stuffing. Then I called our aunt to join us for dinner. Later my mom called and I invited her to dinner, too. We had a nice dinner in the end, and my husband and everyone said it was delicious. Of course, she's the last one to chime in to say it's good since now she is obligated since everyone else said it was good. So, during our grace we thanked God, my mother for the bulgur, my mother-in-law for grating the onions, my brother-in-law for the eggplant, and me for cooking it. My thinking seems petty, but I am now understanding her much more and learning not to try so hard going out of my way, because it doesn't seem to be appreciated. I keep praying to my Lord Jesus and the Holy Spirit to help me through this time. Is this my testing and my pruning? Is this the cross that I must bear and to endure and to care for this woman, who seems down, negative, and comparing everyone; wanting to know where I am; jealous if I am spending time with my mother, aunt or sister; demanding my time and wanting to have breakfast, lunch and dinner with me?

The truth of the matter is that I brought her to my house because if I didn't she may have died as she was not eating, dehydrating, sitting alone in her house. I brought her to my house to alleviate my husband from having to drive out of his way to visit her and to take her grocery shopping or to the doctors. I brought her because I love my Lord and he would want me to care for her and I love my husband who was starting to worry about her. I also brought her to our house to take the burden away from my sister-in-law, who is the only child to her parents who come from Istanbul and live with her most of the year. So again I was thinking of everyone else except myself. I am not a martyr or a saint, just a Christian who is doing what the Spirit led me to do. But I really didn't think it would be this hard. The hardest part is keeping the peace between her and my husband, her own son.

She has a manipulative streak and he knows it. My husband wants to bring it to light, thinking that he can still teach or change an 87-year-old woman. She also has a superficial streak and he knows it and tries to bring that to light. He keeps trying to change her. I advised him to let it go. At 87, she will not change and, guess what, she doesn't want to change. He needs to cut the umbilical cord and understand that her words or actions do not reflect on him. That she is an old woman and this is the way she is, given her life's experiences. She is the best that she's going to be. We can't change her, but we can change our reactions and our response.

So, he has to have more self-control, patience and forbearance. I am praying for that and God's best for us. When she speaks negatively about her own son to me, I tell her that he is my husband and I think he is perfect and that I love him very much and I don't want to hear anything negative about my husband. Matters between her and her son are her own to work out with her own son. My relationship with her son is great and I intend to keep it that way.

My husband feels the same way. We have worked hard to have a loving, God lead family, and a home full of laughter, joy and open discussion. Where my children can feel comfortable in their own home to kick back on the couch, turn on the television, eat anything from the fridge freely as they want, and bring their friends over to do the same. Her house was different with rules and regulations, and don't touch this, and I'll get that for you because you'll mess up the order of things in the refrigerator, and I'll do that because you can't do it. We have brought up our children with confidence knowing that they can achieve anything they desire, that everything we own they own as well, and to enjoy the blessings that the Lord God has provided for us.

When she first moved in, I was going out of my way to be sure she was comfortable and had everything. No matter what we did, she wasn't one to smile. I finally told her that our house is a happy home and it would be nice if she tried to smile and be happy and enjoy life. I finally realized that this is the way she is. She is not an optimist. The glass is always half empty. Her life isn't great no matter what. I am learning not to involve her in everything, because I finally realized that I don't have to worry about it and at 87 she prefers to just sit and mope. So, I'll let her sit and just be as she wishes to be. I have my husband, my children, my mother, and myself along with my sister and nieces and nephews, and my church to be concerned about, I will be concerned about her safety, but not her joy, because some people you just can't make happy. She drains my joy, which bothers me immensely. People comment on how I always smile. My husband and I choose to be happy because we have so many blessings for which we are grateful, predominantly that we have Christ in us and with us and thus we are equally yoked. But when I am with her, she drains my joy. I even brought it up to her more than once that we are a happy family. That she is blessed to have a son who cares for her enough to bring her into his home. Her next words shocked me, "You're the one that wanted me and brought me here, not him." I told her flat out that it was her son's idea because he was concerned about her health and eating habits and depression and I agreed because we both cared, and in all honesty because I love my husband and I love Christ. She obstinately denied his kindness.

I felt dismayed at how a mother could think that way. I realized that she was superficial and very self-centered. Maybe old age does that to someone or that her off thinking is a result of her experience and circumstances. She is my cross that I pray the Lord to lighten the burden. My mother helps. My aunt helps. My sister helps. Praying helps. Exercise helps. Therapy helps. Writing this book helps. Time helps.

Chapter Four

Chinese Food Anyone?

I made the mistake one Saturday morning at breakfast to suggest that maybe this evening we can all get together for Chinese Food. My mother in law loves Chinese Food, especially Kun Pao, the spicier the better. All includes my sister's family and our family and my brother in law's family, and all the elders including my mother-in-law. I regret having mentioned "Chinese Food" as now it became ingrained in my mother-in-law's brain and she was salivating at 9:00 am in the morning. I called my sister to see if she wanted to come over to perhaps do this impromptu casual family get together, but she said that she was tired and her son surprised her by coming home from college, so she wanted to spend time with him. She said perhaps my husband and I will want to go out or come over for coffee later in the evening. I said Ok perhaps we'll do that later.

Now here is the dilemma. My mother-in-law wants and now expects Chinese food. My mother-in-law now expects and wants everyone to gather together. It becomes an unusually uncomfortable situation. My husband asked me, " why did you even mentioned anything? Just let her know when something is completely decided". Now we are in a compromising position. All I want to do is go out of the house with my husband and have a cup of coffee with my sister and brother-in-law, which now becomes a communication monumental nightmare. I have to then explain who is going to be there and why we are not having Chinese food and why she's not coming along.

So in my quick thinking, I went and got Chinese food for lunch for her and our household and explained how others were busy and we are not all going to get together. Later, we said that her son and I are going over my sister's house for coffee.

After we left, she calls my mother, and our aunt, and she didn't find either one home. Then, she calls my sister's house all in panic as to why no one is answering the phone at my mom's or at our aunt's house. She's just doing her Sherlock thing to see if they were with us. Well, they weren't with us. It ended up that my mom had gone to the grocery store and auntie was in the restroom and didn't make it to the phone on time. All this convoluted thinking pattern and clandestine distrusting behavior was really affecting me now, to the point where I had unsettling dreams about it.

Chapter Five

Be Careful What You Pray For

After repeatedly advising my mother-in-law to use her walker or turn on the light in her room when she goes to the bathroom in the middle of the night, she continued to insist on her way in everything. I tried to explain that vanity and shortcuts are not for this time, and that safety and surefootedness are paramount for her safety. I let her know that it would be very difficult for all concerned if she should fall or break something. My husband explained to her in no uncertain terms that she needs to use her walker and wear her appropriate elevated shoes for balance and safety, because we are a two income working family and neither one of us would be able to stay home to care for her.

Of course, she did not listen. Just to set the stage, at this age she seems to lack common sense. Her priorities are skewed. For example, our lovely 90-year-old aunt drove her one day to get her toe nails clipped. The local nail salon with the Vietnamese manicurists charges $5 for that service. Our aunt gets a manicure, while my mother in law gets her toenails clipped. There are several of these nail salons, and they enjoyed trying out different places each month. They came across this one place that was in a two-story building with no elevators and a staircase to the balcony. A manicurists was outside the business, at the bottom of a long staircase, trying to attract business to the second floor. It turns out that they clip toenails for $2 less! So this lady helps my mother in law up the stairs. Envision this: an 87 year old with a cane going up the stairs with the aid of this young Vietnamese woman, while the 90 year old follows behind them. When I heard the story of how she proudly found this place that clips her toe nails for two dollars less, I explained to her that her two dollar savings was nothing in comparison to the jeopardy and risk that she was putting herself, her sister-in-law and our family. I told them that they are not to climb the stairs again and that safety is paramount at this stage. To me, the tradeoff of two dollars was incomprehensible.

It came down to this: instance after instance, fall after fall, and safety discussion after safety discussion, where it became unbearable. My family was continuously under stress, because we had an obstinate person who didn't understand the downside of her actions. I also had to deal with a husband who would not give up and face the fact that this is how his mother is and that she was unwilling to change or relinquish control. It was a difficult situation. I created for myself a sitting, reading, praying and watching television area upstairs in my bedroom, which I termed "my sanctuary".

So one evening, in my sanctuary, I relinquished all control to my heavenly father and my Lord and Savior Jesus. On my knees with arms raised, I told him that I had done what was humanely possible to care for this woman and that I no longer wanted this responsibility. I lamented and asked the Lord to take this heavy yoke as it was beginning to suck the life out of us. The energy that it was taking to be sure that she was safe, that she was eating, that she was happy and not depressed, and that we too had a life and were meeting our other obligations with children, work and other relationships was just too much. I also put in a prayer request for more time with my husband in our home.

My husband, as you know, worked about 80 miles away and with the gas prices as they were and his science experiments being at all hours of the night, he spent four days a week at the university and came home Thursday night or Friday morning for the weekend. So our time together was short and precious. So I prayed for those two things: first that my husband would be with me at home and second, that my mother-in-law would be moving out as the New Year approached. I prayed in the end that He resolves what is best for all concerned in His own way. Praise God! The Lord heard my prayers and his plan unfolded before our eyes.

We were at Thanksgiving dinner over my sister-in-laws house and I expressed my concern to them about the more frequent bladder problem and the falls. Of course, my mother in law conceals all events, so you have to be a detective to get at the truth. For example, my mother in law asks for an aspirin and I asked her if she had pain somewhere. She says her knee is bothering her. I asked if she hit it somewhere or twisted it and where specifically does it hurt? She finally confesses that she fell on her knee. She doesn't use her cane or wear the right slippers, just takes everything for granted. Thank God nothing major happened.

On another occasion, I noticed that she was unable to raise her arm as she was putting dishes away. I asked, " what is the matter with your arm?" She said she slept on it wrong so her muscle was hurting. I saw that her posture was also off and asked to see the back of her shoulder. Well, it was bruised because she had lost her balance. I put some Ben Gay on it and made an appointment with her doctor. I was concerned of the more frequent bladder problem and her losing balance and falling. I had to go to work, so my aunt took her to the doctor. He diagnosed that her B12 was low. I asked her what he said about frequent urination, she said that she didn't bring it up, that she forgot.

The day after Christmas, as I was preparing my daughter to go to the airport at four am in the morning, she fell once more in her room. She had gotten up to go to the bathroom. She, once again, did not use her cane, did not turn on the light and just slipped and fell. We called 911 and sure enough she had broken her thighbone and needed surgery. At the hospital we found out the reason she was losing balance was that she had a urinary tract infection that untreated had gone septic. Most people would have had a burning sensation when going, but because she has diabetes, she didn't feel the burn. In any case, she needed an immediate operation and antibiotics and would need rehabilitation, physical therapy and long-term care.

I told the doctor that there is no one at home to care for her as we both work and she needs assistance with activities like bathing, walking, dressing, and administering her medications and changing catheters and checking her sugar levels. I am not a nurse and I could not do it. So after her rehabilitation, we found the Armenian old age home for her to live. She is so happy now. Even through the storm, the Lord resolved the situation to the benefit of both of us. It took a while to get to the realization that this new place would be her home and that rehabilitation was not going to bring her to the point where she would be independent again and able to go home.

Chapter Six

First Childcare, Now Eldercare

My focus became squarely on eldercare issues in 2007 and 2008, first with my husband's uncle Hank having a stroke and passing away leaving his wife of 42 years behind at age 90 to our oversight. They had no children and she had no local immediate family. Uncle Hank did not want to be bedridden or tube-fed and had expressed that in his Healthcare Initiative and Living Will. So, Auntie Ann and I said a prayer over him after visiting him in the intensive care unit unconscious with the breathing apparatus inserted in him. He went on to Heaven that night. So all the funeral preparations and keeping an eye on his widow was on our shoulders. Thank God my husband's brother came down to help arrange everything. We had a lovely service, funeral and memorial luncheon for Hank reflecting his lifetime of voluntary service as Deacon in the Armenian Apostolic Church. My brother-in-law brought the church choir that he sings with, and we had a beautiful tribute to Hank. He also designed a granite marker in both Armenian and English with beautiful engraving of an Armenian Church.

Fortunately for all, Hank's widow had a driver's license, was healthy, cognizant, self-sufficient, and he taught her to balance a checkbook. Despite all that, she was ninety and needed help with certain issues like car repair or banking, and just ensuring that she is all right each day. Also to be very cautious of solicitors at the door or on the phone and not to provide private information like social security numbers, bank accounts, or information that she is living alone. Their Living Trust was in place.

All was in order. We just needed to ensure that she was safe, not lonely or depressed. The other Armenian ladies in our community were of great assistance by visiting or calling her. She too was very social inviting the ladies for tea or lunch. She also had many friends and some family in Massachusetts, cousins in Fresno, and a nephew in South Carolina who called her on a weekly basis. At her age, she is full of grace and an inspiration to all of us to lead healthy, happy lives full of love and outreach.

My second elder focus was alleviated in that my mother-in-law, now in an Armenian eldercare home that she likes, is also at peace and happy. She is certainly much happier now with individuals caring for her around the clock. There are other residents and visitors of residents who visit with her as well. She is safe and in a good caring environment. Because of her well cared for dietary plan, her diabetes was completely under control. She recites Armenian poetry from memory to the residents when they gather. They even got larger bold print bingo cards for her as she liked to play bingo as her eyesight was getting weaker. I still maintain contact with phone calls or occasional visits but the daily toll and the tension she created in the home, primarily with her own son, vanished. Amen to that!

Visiting her in the Ararat Home in Eagle Rock was fascinating. Because she spoke English and Armenian, the leadership utilized her skills when government inspectors came in to audit the facility, or anytime they needed a translator. There seemed to be a hierarchy in the old age home, as to who sits where or next to whom for activities, TV time or meal times. She felt useful there, somehow "in charge" of the other guests and an interface to the director and attendants. She would let the other guests know if they were getting too loud, or advise them to be patient if they asked for assistance from the caretaker. It seemed like a bit of a soap opera. My husband and I were all good with that as she was happy, the attendants seem to like her, so all is well!

While in the old age home, my moher-in-law lost her younger brother who lived in Istanbul, Turkey. He has visited her in the United States over ten years ago. We did not want to upset her, so we did not let her know when he passed. Time passed, we visited as much as we could. One mother's day, during our visit, she told us that her brother came to her in her dream and was calling her to come. She asked us specifically, if he was alive, we said we had not heard of anything being wrong, so yes he is alive. From that conversation, I knew the time was near.

I recall my own grandmother had that same experience, where a person long passed, in my Grandmother's case it was a nun from the Armenian Convent in Jerusalem, Israel that was near her home, who came to her in a dream and told her it was time for her to come. My grandmother after that dream had a conversation with me letting me know so that I would be prepared in the event of her own passing. I remember she died soon after our conversation.

Similarly, after this conversation with my mother-in-law on Mother's Day, she too passed in her sleep about a week later. It was nice that her grandchildren, nieces and nephews had visited her that weekend also. She passed happy and in peace. She also grew in her knowledge of the Bible and in her faith in Jesus because a pastor came to the old age home on Sundays and provided a sermon and Bible study. At our home, she devoutly prayed and read the Holy Book until her eyes were too weak from macular degeneration. Yet, at the old age home, she learned from the pastor to apply her readings and God's word to real life. Christians are not to worry, not to gossip, not to be envious, and be happy and content in the Lord. I think she finally understood all that!

Chapter Seven

A Boy Named George

I lost my father today, but I am certain that Jesus found him. I know he's in a better place, where there are no insulin shots, no oxygen tubes, no pain, and no need for medication. God gave us a gift, if not many gifts and many miracles. Time and time again with all the 911 calls that my mother had made in an attempt to save my father's life, God gave us more time with him. This last time, it was just too much for my dad. At some point, the good doctors and nurses could not do much and only God can take care of someone and end his suffering. My sister, my mother and I came to a realization, that life in a bed with an oxygen tube, an I.V. and food tube was not what my father wanted in the end. We all went into the chapel and pleaded, implored God with agonizing tears and lamentations for God to take him home to his heavenly mansion and to give him the best room in the house, because my father certainly deserved it.

My father was a generous and compassionate man. He was the kind of man who would give you the shirt off his own back if you said you needed it or if he saw that you needed it. He was the type of soul that helped others. Even stray dogs would find refuge with dad. Even on his deathbed, while the priest gave him his last communion and confession, he insisted on slipping him a hundred dollar bill for his time and kindness. My father has fed the hungry, employed the homeless, given to family members in times of financial shortage. He extends himself out without hesitance to help others, to show generosity and kindness to others. He unconditionally accepts and loves everyone. I have never heard him say an unkind word to or about anyone. He strives to make people feel special, appreciated and loved. Even those who have hurt him or taken advantage of his kindness, he doesn't curse or have vengeance on them. Instead, he prays for them and prays that God will reveal himself to them and shows them even more kindness. In other words, my Dad always takes the high road of forgiveness and love.

My father knew Jesus. On his last outing outside the nursing home in his electric wheel chair, I walked alongside him across the street to the non-denominational Christian church. There was a festival going on and I thought it would be fun for him to get out into the beautiful air and listen to music and young people dancing and singing. However, it took so much time to get him ready with all his paraphernalia, his catheter & urine bag, his oxygen tank, getting him dressed, and then he had to have a bowl movement, by the time we got across the street the music was over and the musicians had already left. I asked one of the church ladies if there were any musicians or singers left that could play a song, she said unfortunately they had left. Then she leaned closer to Dad and said would you like to say a prayer together. He said yes, and I agreed that a prayer together would be greatly appreciated. So this lovely sister in Christ knelt down next to my father asked him his name and then asked him if he knew Jesus. Dad said with a big smile "Of course, I know and love Jesus!" We held hands and prayed in the parking lot praising the Lord and asking for his grace and mercy for health and healing. That was my father's last excursion other than when he was taken to emergency, then to intensive care, then to another nursing home, then again to emergency and intensive care and then to heaven.

I'll never forget the morning I was working in my office and my mother called and said that Dad has told the doctor that he is ready to go to God. That he no longer wanted intrusive or aggressive efforts to prolong his life. It shocked me. My father was not a quitter. He was literally a fighter and a survivor. Anytime you asked him how he's doing, despite his pain and all his medications and his immobility, his response would be in Armenian, "Bombayee bes em!" translation "I am dynamite!" His mother passed away during childbirth when my father was four years of age and, thereafter, his father took to drinking and would be gone for weeks. Therefore, his grandparents and his uncles' families brought up my father.

At age fourteen, with street smarts and entrepreneurial vigor he started a photography business (a room, a chair, a camera). He learned photography as an unpaid apprentice to a photographer. Thereafter, wherever war or blizzard took him around the world, he opened a studio and worked and fed himself and his family. At the end, he knew many languages, four fluently. In his deathbed, I heard my dad converse with one of the Jewish doctors in Hebrew. I knew he knew Hebrew, but I didn't know he knew it better than English. He was fluent in Hebrew, Armenian, Turkish and Arabic. He could pass for his business needs as a photographer in Greek, Spanish, Indian, Philippine and Farsi. Although he has been a newspaper, wedding, and portrait photographer, as he got older he settled on immigration and passport photography. In this way, when a customer came to his studio, he made them feel welcome in the United States by speaking their language.

So for my father to say that he had enough and wanted to go to God was out of character. I immediately dropped what I was doing, and went to the hospital to see what was happening. So many times before we thought he was dying and he had pulled through. Surely, he would come through this time as well. And he always said he was dynamite, and that he wanted to live. He had a fighting spirit. This time he looked at us with a smile and said, "I gave it all I've got." In his youth, my dad had taken up amateur boxing as a sport. He always enjoyed watching Mohammed Ali, George Foreman, Nathaniel Holyfield fights on television and cable. His least favorite fight was the one-second fight that we had all gathered to watch on pay per view cable and it ended with a knock out punch as soon as it started. My father tagged Tyson as "a selfish savage" with no sportsmanship and no desire to entertain or please the public or his fans. Dad told mom that he clearly saw his grandmother Lucia and grandfather Abraham sitting in the chair in the corner of his room, telling him it is time to come home.

I believe my dad felt that he had fought his illnesses long enough. The doctors told him that in order to keep breathing; he would now need a tracheotomy and a breathing machine in place of his biped mask and oxygen tank. Dad never wanted to be tied down or bed ridden as he was now. My father was a free spirit, a ballroom dancer like Fred Ester, a comedian and lover of life. He loved being where the action is, amongst the people. Every New Years Eve he would take the 4 hour train ride from Massachusetts to New York to be in Times Square. When we moved to the West Coast, after New Year's Eve, he would drive to Los Angeles for the Rose Bowl Parade, always camera ready.

I also believe that he saw how his illness was now affecting my mother. In her deep love and desire to care for her husband of 48 years, in the last 15 years of their marriage, she was his caretaker. In this last year, however, he became less mobile and needed assistance even with toileting and she assisted his 280 pound frame, and exasperated her back and hip. She may have had latent issues from a prior auto accident, aggravated and manifested as arthritis in her back, hip and leg.

My mother and father truly loved each other. She didn't want to let him go, refusing to accept hospice guidelines of not calling 911 when he passes out. Hospice had to take him off the program. He also did not want to leave her behind alone. We had to reassure him that she would not be alone, that we would be there for her and that it would be OK to relinquish his soul to God's care. My mom's arthritis pain hurt so much, that she now needed a walker with a seat so that if the pain was too much she can just sit. Her sitting by his bedside at the nursing home knitting for hours on end did not help with her joint flexibility either. Seeing mom with a walker, burnt out from caring for him saddened Dad. He loved my mother so much. On his deathbed, he told my mom "I would die for you." When my mom saw him suffering, she finally relinquished control of him to the Lord and prayed that the Lord will take him to his care and end his pain.

As for me, I spent time reading him passages from the Bible. I laid hands on his head while saying the Lord's Prayer, and the Hail Mary. Talked to him about the many rooms in God's mansion and how we made reservations for him through prayer for the best room God has for my dad. We talked about how finally he will reunite with his mother and other family members. He joked, "If it's nice up there, I won't come back."

We talked about how salvation was assured through his faith in Jesus, and through God's sacrifice on the cross and his resurrection and that through His blood our sins are forgiven. Because his mother died when he was four, he had this low self-esteem. He took care of others, but didn't take care of his own body. Deep down, he harbored a misunderstanding that his mother left him because he wasn't "a good boy". I explained to him that God forgives everything, and that we are all sinners and it is through God's grace and mercy, and Christ's death and resurrection that we are saved. I believe he understood that when our priest administered and my father received his last rights and communion. I stroked his hand and forehead, sang our Gregorian hymns, and soothing Christmas carols and read Psalm 23 to keep him in peace. Believe it or not, in the midst of all this, I had my laptop in the intensive care room and was loading cost basis information for a client's security positions so that their yearend reporting on long term and short term realized gains and losses would be accurate. That was just too surreal. The mundane task may have eased my nerves through this soul-searching, gut wrenching emotional ordeal. Thereafter, it made me decide that financial planning was not the field for me any longer.

My father requested what we now know was his infamous "last meal". The doctors had removed his tubing as he requested with the exception of a pain killer. He asked for a hamburger and some soup. For lack of time and energy, we went to the hospital cafeteria and got what he wanted. We also got him chocolate pudding and some butter cookies because as a diabetic he always had a sweet tooth. He was so cute, savoring each bite of his hamburger. He asked my sister to feed him the chocolate pudding with the spoon upside down so he can lick the inside of the spoon. Then, like the cookie monster on Sesame Street, he asked if there was another cookie. We laughed at all his quirkiness, yet knowing full well what we were experiencing was in all probability his last meal. It's almost like the flesh is having a last little celebration before calling it quits.

My father had COPD (Cardio Obstructive Pulmonary Disorder) brought on by thirty years of smoking. Even though he had quit when his grandchildren were born, the damage to his lungs had already taken hold. He also had late onset diabetes, because he refused to follow good eating habits and control his sweet and caloric intake. The medications, inhalers, oxygen that prolonged his life just couldn't prolong it anymore. It came to a point that his body filled with fluid, and his blood pressure was falling. If they administer lasix to take out the fluid, his blood pressure would fall further. They were giving him dopamine to keep his blood pressure up, without the dopamine the blood pressure fell. His back was to the corner and there were no options left. The doctors continued his oxygen and started him on morphine to ease the respiratory problem so that he would not be in pain. He passed peacefully while we were at his side. We knew his spirit had left his body. He looked so at peace. We raised the volume on the church choir music that we had brought along, and hugged each other and talked affirmations to his spirit, the angels and the Lord whose presence we clearly felt was in the room with us.

Chapter Eight

2009 Recession – What Next?

I am writing this chapter in the family room of my mother's home. The succession of events that lead me here are probably quite common right now, as many individuals have lost jobs, businesses have closed doors as the banks came tumbling down. Who saw this coming? The top management of major home lending institutions and investment banks saw it coming, although they want to claim their innocence. They saw it coming, because they had solid investments placed with shorts on the hope and anticipation of the falling housing market. They insured the fall because they also made money on the sale and packaging of the NINA (no income no asset) loans, Zero Documentation and Stated Income Loans, sub-prime loans to substandard credit holders. They stood to make money from both the initial sales and then the increase or demise of the housing and mortgage industry. They did this without full disclosure, with no regard to ethics or their fiduciary duties; all for greed! So the shrapnel went to the individual mortgage holders, then to the small businesses who depended on their small lines of credit and their customers' ability to purchase. All of that crumbled, while the heads of Fannie Mae and Freddie Mac and Goldman Sachs, AIG and others stood to make millions and hundreds of thousands as bonuses.

After my father's passing, I found it emotionally difficult to discuss death and disability issues such as life insurance, long-term care insurance or estate planning. My heart was no longer in it and it was too close to heart and home to objectively do my job as a financial planner. With the attention to first Hank's death, then my father's passing, my pipeline had dried up. I opted to go back to a steady salaried position and took a position as Controller for a family-run residential construction business. Not knowing construction, I researched and educated myself on the nuances of construction estimating, costing, and accounting in order to do well for the interview.

I accepted the position as controller for a firm that built structural steel for the high-end homes along the California coast. I really enjoyed my first year, working with the crew and doing all aspects of office management, accounting, financial and strategic planning. After celebrating Christmas 2008, in a matter of three months all the projected bids we had out and people who had signed contracts for jobs could no longer find financing. The banks closed our small business credit line for no apparent logical reason, other than their own illiquidity, and left us out to dry. The owners were now funding the business from their own personal wealth and how many payrolls could they realistically fund? I told the owners that in affect they could no longer afford the payroll, including myself. We had already taken a 5% cut in January, then up to 10% by March, but by end of April business and financing had dried up and the government was talking about a global economic crash, averting another great depression. It began with Lehman Brothers bankruptcy. Then AIG, the world's largest insurer, who the government felt could not fall, and they had to prop up. Then the banks began to fail one by one as people failed to make housing payments and foreclosures started rising. The government stepped in with the Bank Bail Out program.

Soon after, the auto industry came to a screeching halt with gas prices high and people now fearing the loss of jobs, loss of homes, and loss of American lifestyle. The government put out the "Cash for Clunkers" program to stimulate auto sales to curtail a potential downward spiral to impact other related industries like steel that go into building an auto. With the same program, they wanted to get old gas guzzling cars off the roads with the hopes of replacing them with newer economic environmentally friendly models. The unions, who put the administration in power through collective campaign financial support, were now getting the government support.

The government began the Home Affordability program to salvage people from foreclosures and to encourage banks to modify the loans. But like any well-intentioned government program, it works at a snail's pace and has low impact. Banks were slow to modify or not modifying at all at the whim of the investors behind the loans. Once mortgagers are behind in payments, banks don't accept partial payments even if homeowners want to pay, getting them further into the hole. Bank Owned signs and Foreclosure signs, empty homes spotted practically every street and community in America, causing home values in general to fall. The government stepped in and gave a first-time homeowner credit to stimulate the housing market and help move sales of the foreclosure inventory.

Of course, new home sales and new construction stopped, creating a job loss in the construction industry. So the government came along with a "stimulus package" to slow down further job loss, to rebuild America's infrastructure roads, bridges, schools, etc., so as to provide some construction union jobs. Government jobs were abundant now, with the FDIC hiring forensic auditors, so they can audit all the banks that the government had given Bank Bail Out money. The employment office (EDD) was hiring, to process all the layoffs and job losses and unemployment paperwork. The IRS was hiring to audit all the people that are utilizing all the tax credits and the complexities of the stimulus and tax changes that ensued.

But the private sector was dormant…no jobs…no capital investment…just hunkering down as no crystal ball could tell as to where the economy and government regulation, intervention and taxation were going. The government now had Czars to check on compensation! Government had fingers everywhere as they were supposedly "helping" to prop up everything! As government was spending, China was lending, the American patriots began revolting against big government, big taxes, and big unions who now seemed to have the government in their pockets. The balance between the public versus the private sector compensation, benefits and pension had tipped the wrong way. Teachers, firefighters, police, government employees, and the people you trust and depend on were now demanding more and more and if they don't get their demands they were walking off the jobs and protesting violently in union cohesiveness. The non-union sector is subsidizing the union pensions in effect through a heavier tax burden. Then the Healthcare bill was passed and was duly dubbed by Vice President Biden, as "A Big Fucking Deal" that basically screws everybody. The rest remains to be seen. The slump continued with more people going on food stamps, the national debt doubling and no possible end to this malaise of an economy.

Having lost my job as a construction controller, and looking at a barren job market, and having depleted my savings during my job search, we decided to rent out my home and move in with my mother. My mom was lonely after Dad's passing. My daughter was now away at college and my husband stayed by his work for four days a week, so it just made sense for my son and me to be at mom's house through this time. It took a year to finally give up and take any job opening available which was a seasonal holiday position as a cosmetic beauty advisor for Estee Lauder at Macy's. A position, I had held over 10 years ago at an hourly wage less than 20 years ago, plus commission.

It was like reliving my youth and getting a second chance at life. That's how it felt. There were still familiar faces of those that had worked for me when I was the Estee Lauder Counter manager. My life was replaying in front of me. I knew if I worked hard and proved that I still had the sales skills, if a position became available the store manager, who knew my capabilities and liked me, would provide the promotion. I also knew God was watching out for me and had a plan, so my part was to do the best I could each day. So my motto is to walk with God, day by day, and leave the controls to Him. There was no other choice at this time. I woke up each morning and asked God what was on the agenda and I did as He said. With everything gone…His voice was clear…maybe because I was listening and leaving it all up to Him.

In a matter of three months, the seasonal position converted to a part time permanent position. Then in a few months, I was offered a full time permanent position as the Elizabeth Arden Counter Manager. The line needed someone to build the business and clientele, and I did exactly that with events and customer relationship building. Soon, biding my time, and doing a great job in the position I was in, I finally was offered a position as the Fine Jewelry Manager, a salaried position with a percentage override of the department sales. Although it made only half of my controller salary, I was just grateful to the Lord that I had a salaried position and excited to manage a team once again to have an impact on the business.

As soon as I got the position, I told mom I was going back to my home so that I could try to modify my loan and try for the Home Affordability government program to reduce my payments to 31% of our new household income. To do the program, you have to be residing in the home as your primary residence. As it stands, the mortgage plus property taxes are now at about 55% of our lower income. I figured if I don't try, I might not be able to ever afford to go back into the home. I didn't want to be at mom's house forever. The day after I moved in, I filled out the thirty-page package with documentation of pay stubs, bank statements, taxes, hardship letter, and family budget. A year later, into the expanding hole of back mortgage payments plus interest and late fees, I am still waiting on the loan modification results. That's government work for you. But, I love my job and I love being back in my home.

My daughter finished her post baccalaureate in Sciences and has been accepted to Columbia University for Masters of Science in Nutrition, aiming to be a Registered Dietitian. My son is graduating high-school and plans to go to a community college for his general education then transfer to a university.

My son is adamant not to be in debt. He is seeing the debt debacle that his friends and the country's education system lures you into with student loans. He opted to go to a community college, commute from home, and pay for his own education. After his general education, he transferred to a Cal State University. He continued to work two part time jobs and I paid for the balance when needed.

Other than hanging by a thread, waiting on the loan modification, my husband is gainfully employed. Life is good. We are peacefully waiting with great expectation on the Lord and the Bank!

Chapter Nine

Visitation

My husband got the opportunity to go back to Istanbul, his birthplace, to attend a Science Symposium to share one of his scientific findings. Never in a million years did he think he would ever go back to Turkey. He was a child when his parents decided to immigrate to the United States, sponsored by his uncle Hank and his new wife Ann. So not having served in the Turkish military, we feared repercussions of going back, even with full US citizenship and a US passport. In order to take this trip, my husband visited the Turkish Consulate in Las Angeles. With Turkey wanting to be part of the European Economic Union, they greeted my husband with open arms, and the consulate provided him with a special letter of invitation signed by the Consulate himself. He entered and exited Istanbul with no questions asked.

Visiting his old neighborhood and old school was amazing. He had expected big changes, but much of the past remained the same. What seemed in his old youthful memory to be large vast streets where he played outside for hours, were now looking like old narrow streets. The best part of his trip was to visit his Uncle Stephan and cousin Ani and her family. This was his mother's brother, Stephan's daughter. Stephan lost his wife Suzan to cancer. Upon my husband's departure from Istanbul, at age 10, on the ship Christopher Columbus headed to Ellis Island, Suzan had reminded him not to forget his cousin Ani in Istanbul. My husband felt that calling rushing upon him during his visit.

Ani's son, Ari, was coming of age for mandatory Turkish military service. He was an artist, like my mother-in-law and Stephan, both having artistic talents that ran in the genes on my husband's side. Ari loved to draw and wanted to work in the video gaming industry drawing characters, heroes, villains and monsters, for video games. There was no such industry in Istanbul. He wanted to try to make his move in America. After speaking with me, my husband and I decided that we would welcome Ari to our home at such time that we returned to it in order to assist him in pursuing his artistic dreams. God placed this in both my husband's and my heart to help Ari to pursue the American dream.

No sooner than moving back into our home, we got word from Ani that her son Ari got accepted to an American Language school in San Diego and would be coming out for a six-month program to strengthen his English language skills. Our plan was to enable him to perhaps show case his work on his website and start applying to various animation and video companies that may see his art skills and would want to pull the paper work for a workers visa to keep him in the United States. It was a long shot, but postponing military service in the Turkish army was also a strong motivation.

The Lord had already been working on Ari's heart in having a closer relationship with Him. Ari got acclimated quickly. He began attending a nearby non-denominational church where he hoped he could meet people that may assist him in his desire to stay in America. Ari, in his mid twenties, had no need to drive a car in Istanbul, but after using the transport system going back and forth to the language school and walking to most anywhere else started making an effort to get his driver's license. Social circles were limited here, but he did try to connect through our Armenian Church with some old friends that he had known at one time in Istanbul.

We wrote resumes and he sent out many in response to art ads. I also impressed upon him that he needed to be drawing and putting up fresh content on his website as his resume was sending potential employers to that website. But he missed home and being the only son he missed mom and Ani missed him. Rather than putting up fresh new content that would impress potential employers, he Skyped with his family and friends in Turkey, for literally hours every night. It became evident that finding a company to sponsor him would be really difficult and that he wasn't stepping out enough, making a social circle, and nothing was going to change for him while Skyping in his room every night.

The language school was coming to an end, as was his student visa, and to renew it would cost additional tuition money to perhaps a video gaming school. His parents would not be able to continue on that path and we were not in any position to assist having been recently unemployed, and waiting on the loan modification in order to save our primary residence. In the end, he had to return to Turkey and did do his military service.

Our understanding is not as great as the Lord's, so perhaps there was a season of time that my husband and I were to commit to Ani and her son Ari. I believe he was made a better person and grew from the experience of being in America for the year that he spent with us. One thing, hopefully, he gathered is how hard Americans work. Regrettably, both my husband and I hardly had spare time or money to entertain or travel or tour with him. Hopefully, he learned it takes hard work and dedication to achieve anything in this world. Perhaps that was the life lesson that God wanted to impart on him. Or perhaps God wanted to impart to him how wonderful his home in Istanbul with his family and friends really was, and to be appreciative of that. All in all, my son also benefited from having a big brother around to talk and laugh with and to play video games with. So, in the end, we both benefited from the time together and knowing our family in Istanbul. Perhaps God helped us save our home, because of the hospitality we showed Ari despite the financial hardships we were trying to overcome.

Chapter Ten

2012 – Modification

One morning, back in our new home, after over one year of faxing documents and more documents, I open the door to go to work and there is a foreclosure notice and auction date taped with blue tape on my front door! My heart started racing! I had provided all the information, time and time again, and thought we were nearing the modification conclusion! I tore down the notice and called the HUD counselor. They forwarded me to HOPE an organization that handled the execution of the Home Affordability Modification Program (HAMP). They called the lender on a three-way call and the attorney on the foreclosure notice and asked why the foreclosure was preceding when the documents were submitted. They pressed with several questions and to my relief and delight were able to postpone the foreclosure for 30 days to conclude the modification. By the grace of God, and this non-profit home counseling organization, I was able to get the loan finally modified. I had to call each week, sometimes twice or three times, to ensure all was well with the docs. Finally, in mid-2012, we were on a three-month trial plan to complete the modification!

Regardless of the modification, these were stringent times. New terminologies came into play such as "under-employed", which describes my situation. Now making half what I used to make, our budget was tighter than ever. I put myself back on credit counseling to ensure we could pay off the credit cards and not incur late fees or high interest rates. So when the car had problems, payments to other people like the dentist, the doctor, the water bill or the electric bill or the car payment fell behind. It was like playing musical chairs or leapfrog with who do we pay next. Car repairs, vacations, and other non-essentials were postponed, or we did it ourselves like the landscaping, haircuts, plumbing repairs. We watched pennies postponing the watering of the grass for as long as we could, turning off lights, and not using heating or air-conditioning opting to be in layered sweaters instead. We stopped eating out and converting to a more-or-less vegetarian diet which was actually healthier, too. These are small changes that accumulate to a lot of savings in hard times. In lean times, we need to "hunker down" and reassess where our money is going and prioritize what is important.

We wanted to avoid a bankruptcy at all cost. Although we spoke with a bankruptcy attorney about twice in this past three-year period and had documents ready in the event that lenders pushed us to that level, and with that foreclosure notice I was close to putting up that bankruptcy protection. Yet, it's not clear that it would have worked, as I had my unsecured lenders on a consumer protection plan anyway, most of the debt I had was the mortgage. A bankruptcy on your record really for a lifetime and 10 years on the credit report, didn't seem worth it. I decided to keep witling away at the unsecured debt with as little payments as possible, and used the windfalls, gifts, commission checks, bonuses for reducing and eliminating that debt.

In its place, my husbands and my student loans, and our PLUS loans (for my daughters undergraduate studies)+ are now past the forbearance and deferment stages and must be paid. So, I am making the smallest monthly payments I possibly can on student loan debt, which is the income based graduated repayment plan. If it's not one thing, it is another. Sometimes, I wonder if the Amish have it right. All these self-help books say, "De-clutter and simplify your life." Recently, I have found the cell phone as my worst enemy #1. Regardless of where I am or what I am doing, it creates immediate access to me. Remember when voicemail first came out, we thought it was a Godsend. You could choose to listen or not listen to your voicemail or delete it. People expect immediate access to you with the cell phone, even on vacation, because it is with you and it is always on. They text you or they call you or leave a voicemail, they expect that it is where you are! So the deserted island with no reception sounds fabulous about now! For some reason, everyone is expected to have a cell phone now.

Therapists tell you to build parameters, or fake walls, rules of engagement with various people to allow or not allow access or to allow access on your terms. If everyone had his or her own rules of engagement or had a "self-protective" philosophy, no one would be able to get along with anyone. Whatever happened to loving open arms and consideration of "others' " feelings and mutually respectful relationships? The social norms or proper etiquette of being nice to seniors, or to women have been eradicated with the concept that everyone is equal and nobody should be treated special. The whole concept of social justice has come full circle to injustice for all. People can't go around thinking, "I deserve this" regardless of what effort I put out. We all came into the world as babies and we do the best we can in the environment, the background, and the people around us to succeed. Everyone has some limitations social, physical, mental, financial, and spiritual. The beauty of the human brain and spirit, especially in America, is that we all can succeed and utilize our best talents and overcome any limitations to achieve success. We can succeed by putting out effort, taking risk, working hard and smart, being creative, resourceful, researching and learning to achieve and bring to reality the desires of our heart. We engage with others through partnerships and teams. We leverage what we know and have developed through patents on intellectual property, franchising or employing others by building a business.

Chapter Eleven

Hip Hop

Ann fell this morning and broke her hip. My daughter sends me a text that says, "Mom, I am dying". And my son said he dropped two classes in college because one he didn't like the teacher and the other because he is changing his major. The roller coaster is escalating once again. It is the middle of the retail season; we are all prepping for the biggest retail day of the year, Black Friday, the day after Thanksgiving. I have peanut butter stuck all over my hands dealing with sandwich issues once again.

I had a Sunday off at last! My husband went off to play soccer with a local over-fifty league. I decided to go to church. This is a local non-denominational Christian church where my son had been invited by a friend to attend a youth group meeting. My son liked the group, the youth pastor and the bible study. We discovered this local church when my son invited my husband and me to go to church with him. I thought if my teenager wants to go to church, then by all means my husband and I are going to go! I went to the morning service, which was packed, and I was looking for an empty seat. I saw a lady with an open aisle seat next to her. I took a second take and she was one of my daughter's girl-scout troop leaders from over 15 years ago! I went and stood next to her, tapped her on the shoulder and we were both surprised and delighted. She was looking great and we stood and worshiped the same Jesus together. That was awesome. After the service, we took a few minutes to catch up and exchange cell phone numbers.

Right after church, pulling out of the parking lot, I get a phone call from my brother-in-law that Ann fell and he was at her house waiting for the paramedics. She needed immediate surgery and about a month of rehab and then will use a walker in all likelihood. She lives alone and would require care. So I called my sister-in-law who is a retired pharmacist, with her own two aging parents living with her, and told her the situation. We discussed how to help Ann who has no children of her own to maintain her independence and still stay safe. Thanks to my sister-in-law who stepped up and came to Ann's aid. She helped a lot regarding medications, and moved her to the assisted living rehabilitation center we selected. Ann was so adamant to go back to her home. She took her rehab very seriously and wanted out in 30 days. She could have stayed another month or so, but she told the rehab center she wanted to go home.

Problem is both my sister-in-law and my hands are full. She with her aging parents, and me with my full-time job and my young adults while my husband works four days away from home. So we quickly went looking for someone who could live with her to cook, clean, and bathe her and take her to doctor appointments, grocery shopping and be a companion for her so she doesn't fall or hurt herself in any way. We found an Armenian caretaker, a referral through the circles of friends that my mother had. These are friends that she knew in elementary school in Jerusalem, who now are in America, with whom she has kept in touch with. Her friend had an operation and this caretaker lived with her while she re-cooperated. They had kept her number in the event that they needed her again. Thank goodness Ann had the financial means to hire a live in. She was concerned of the night with the frequency that she got up to go to the bathroom. This caregiver and the timeliness of discovering her was heaven sent. Plus, she spoke and cooked Armenian! On the days that she had off, I hired a local friend who is a care provider for another elderly couple about three times a week. I had met her through University of California San Diego, Stein Institute for Research on Aging (SIRA) where I had served as a member of the Community Board of Advisors. We had round the clock care after she came home from rehab.

We also ordered the "I have fallen and can't get up" medical alert button service for additional peace of mind, Ann's and ours. I modified the bathroom by adding a couple of bars so she could safely step in and out of the shower without falling per advice from the occupational therapist who visited her at home a few times after her surgery. Between the physical therapist, the occupational therapist and the two caregivers and the button Ann was well taken care of, and we could continue with our lives and readdress needs as they came up.

Some of the events that needed my assistance are filing federal and state taxes. At some point in your life, after having worked and paid your taxes, you would think at age 95 you can stop having to file or pay taxes. If the government is deducting from your social security for Medicare, can't they just take the taxes out and send you a net check and be done with it. If you already have enough retirement savings, why can't the affluent opt out of receiving social security checks and have it be converted to treasury bonds (such as available thru treasury direct at the Federal Reserve Bank) in their names for their heirs or beneficiaries or be donated to the general social security fund. Why can't the government look for efficient and streamlined ways to save money or social security? Why does every government solution have to be complex and mired in government regulation, paperwork, and bureaucracy? It's called job security. They create built in inefficiency and waste so that government can stay large and look busy, and suck resources in the form of payroll and pensions, while leaving private sector tax payers lurched and out to dry.

Another issue that came up is Ann's refusal to bathe. When people get older, bathing seems to become a chore or a fear. In this case, she did not want to bathe because she was afraid of catching a cold. Older people watch television where everything seems sensationalized and they think they are at risk. Going out to get the flu shot becomes paramount and the fear of not getting the flu shot and getting the flu scares them. So I talked with her and the caretaker and said let's set up a schedule of bathing twice a week. Let's do it an hour after lunch in the warmth of the day. Run the shower so it will be steamy and hot, raise the heat in the house if necessary, and bathe mid afternoon. Let's put it on the calendar for Mondays and Thursdays, and let callers know that you are occupied at those certain times, so they can visit later in the day.

We also had to address Ann's financial concerns. With the downturn in the economy in 2008 and our slow uneventful recovery now going on five years in 2013, seniors like Ann and my mother are feeling the pinch. Their savings are earning nothing. At their age, the strategy these hard working, saving, frugal lifestyle generation, was safety of principle, live on social security and the interest on their investments, and leave an inheritance. They are following a self-less noble financial strategy, still using coupons, looking for the sales, searching for the highest CD rates. Yet, zero interest rates on their savings, doubled with inflation on their gas, utilities, food and prescription medication, has them "eating away at their principle" which is against the fiber of their conscience. My first thought about not bathing was the extent of her frugality and her expressed fear of running out of money before the natural end of her life.

To appease her financial concerns, I had her do a little math and explained to her that Bernanke, the Chairman of the Federal Reserve Bank, said that he may start raising interest rates in 2015 only two years from now. That he was keeping interest rates artificially low today because of all the people that lost their jobs, and are still losing homes due to foreclosure and others whose debt on the homes are over the value of the homes. He is giving people the chance to refinance and to save or sell their homes with low interest rates. So, this is a short-term issue and everything that goes down eventually goes up and interest rates will come up again. Then I calculated her monthly budget and divided it into her total savings and expressed how long her money would last, safely over age 100. She laughed and said "God I hope I don't live to 100!" She reminded me how her cousins passed in bed in their own home at age 98. I also told her not to worry about inheritance, she worked hard and saved money for this time in her life when she retired and couldn't work and that is what the "save for a rainy day" money is for. She now needs her caretaker, which is a great use of her savings. The caretaker's cost was another issue growing in her mind as her budget basically doubled with a live in caregiver. Praise God that she and uncle Hank had the foresight and the wherewithal to save for their senior independence. Ann is doing fine with her walker and her caretaker!

Chapter Twelve

Female Bonding

In the business world, women form a bond. Often it is a mutually supportive bond, like group therapy, by which they can help each other to address a myriad of issues that confront women on a daily basis with their home relationships. Mundane or routine questions like how your weekend was or how your day off was can spew off into a laundry list of issues, problems, occurrences, needs, tasks that are on their plate or that they had to overcome. When you are in the sandwich generation with peanut butter all over your hands, a day off is more like time to tend to your home and family, often a more demanding job. The day is consumed with catching up with life, the laundry, the cleaning, the grocery shopping, paying bills, and planning of weekly meals, events, and appointments. Depending on the physicality of your job, it sometimes is just collapsing on the couch or crashing in bed with your sore back, legs, arms or migraine. This day off time is spent tending to the needs of others like your husband, children, parents and in-laws. Then thanking God that you have a job you can go back to where you get some sanity back, adult speak, peace or fun, that is, if you enjoy your job. Your day off was definitely not restful and relaxing.

From the perspective of a female manager who manages other women, you walk the line of providing comfort and understanding versus towing the line of tasks and productivity. The understanding is that despite all of us having challenges, we can all sit and gripe or moan, or we can muster the energy to get the work at hand done. As a manager, we cannot discount the needs of the business due to varying priorities or demands on employees outside of the office. As a female employer or manager, employees anticipate that you will be more compassionate and empathetic than you would have to be compared to male counterparts. Often, they would not share their problems and issues with the male manager as they readily do with the female manager. If the female manager works like the male manager, perhaps reserving compassion or understanding, then she is not so endearingly termed "the bitch". As a good manager, you can try to accommodate schedules or flexible work hours, but one has to be mindful of the overall needs of the business, its customers' needs, and the impact on other employees as well. The business has goals and customers need to be serviced or you could all be out of a job if we lose focus on revenues, profits and reputation.

Once we step into the workplace, home needs to be left behind and inversely once we are home, work has to be left behind. Often, this is easier said than done. Finding the balance and being resilient enough to bounce between the demands of work and the home is what defines a woman's success. Another equally important determinant of her success is the support that she has with childcare, eldercare, and self-care that comes from her support circle: spouse, friends, family, neighbors, church, and community groups and services, and even employer programs.

The cell or mobile phone, which everyone relies on, has become a form of frequent communication. The calls and texts are infiltrating and blurring the woman's work versus home time differentiation. From my vantage point as a working mom and a manager of other women, if there is an urgent matter or emergency, it is more often the woman's cell phone that is the point of contact rather the father's phone. The translation of "urgent" has been watered down as well. It can be "we are out of milk" or "grandma hasn't picked me up from school yet" or "are you off work today?". To curtail this, one has to create the parameters and it varies from the family needs.

The respect of time has diminished with the heightened use of the cell-phone. The expectation of not receiving the message has diminished. People who send messages or texts via cell phone are expecting immediate responses, and the recipient is feeling the need or urgency to immediately respond. This is an odd circumstance and difficult to manage as the children need help, elder parents need help, other employers have questions if holding two jobs, study groups are communicating if you are in school, alerts are being sent from your bank account, investment accounts, credit protection agencies, school districts…the list goes on and on.

Turn off the phone and get to work. We just can't turn the damn thing off anymore and everyone is expected to be in reach anytime anywhere, except at church perhaps! Proper phone etiquette is so important and society has not developed such a protocol as of yet, although many have tried. If you are with someone, in a meeting or at lunch or on a date, concentrate on the person who has given up their precious time to be with you. Make that interaction count. The selfie craze is overdone as well. How many pictures do you need together that are in the cloud? Do other people really want to know what you are eating for breakfast, lunch or dinner. Unless it is your job, like you are a cook, nutritionist, or food critic, whom are you trying to impress?

Here is a sample of women working together supporting each other thru life's demands and issues: one may have a disabled husband and she is the primary earner. Another may be a single mother with children with a MIA ex-husband who provides no child support, or one who provides some financial support plus has the children every other weekend. Another female employee may be living with her elderly widowed mother who has Alzheimer. Another employee works but is suffering from symptoms of MS or cancer or another chronic disease that limits her working hours or disables her at unforeseen times. Another is contemplating surgery or just went thru surgery and rehab and has limitations as to what she can do. Another, has no childcare resources or family or trusting relationships to leave her children, or has to pick up her children from school at a certain time. If the children are sick, she is the care provider as her husband works and earns more so he wouldn't be expected to leave his work.

Everyone in a team is dependent on the other team members. When one member is suffering, it affects the team morale. The productivity of the missing employee as well as those working to do both their work and her duties suffer. The work team becomes your extended family where one can vent frustration; get helpful advice or direction on how to handle a situation and to whom to turn. Company work and life balance counseling, as an Employee Assistance Program, provide information and referral services on wellness, financial, legal and grief resources. Programs such as these assist management and employees as a method to workout issues. This resource allows the manager to refer the employee to address the issues that she would otherwise be addressing on the shop floor or office lunch room. The manager can then focus on the needs of the business and feel comfortable with the referral as a knowledgeable source. Plus, it offers the manager a healthy detachment from the employees' private circumstances. We absolutely care about our employees' well being. We can listen, hand them a tissue, perhaps give a hug if appropriate or pray with them or for them, and share advice if we have gone thru the same circumstance, but it is good practice to refer them to a professional who can address their matter more fully and accurately.

51

practice to refer them to a professional who can address their matter more fully and accurately.

Chapter Thirteen

Anxiety

People around me are complaining of heart palpitations, stress, migraines and anxiety. This includes my employees, mother, sister, and now my daughter. She calls crying over the phone. She is having a panic attack and she is on her roof top patio at her New York City apartment in Manhattan trying to get fresh air and to breath. She is getting a masters in nutrition at Columbia University. It's hard to console her from California over the phone. I ask her to use slow breathing techniques and think happy thoughts and count her blessings. That life and God's been good to her. Why would she think He would fail her now? She is concerned about getting into a dietetic internship, not knowing where and how to pay for it. So we go thru the analysis of each option, pros and cons, and do the necessary research.

I tell her sometimes we can't control it all. We can plan as best we can, but what other forces are at work as to what unfolds is uncertain. This is the mystery of life and faith, hard work, optimism and anticipation. Often, you have to put your foot in the Jordan River, as a leap of faith in God, and watch it part in front of you and follow the path that it leads. During the day, I sent her encouraging texts and voicemails, which probably translated to annoying her. Then in the evening, I sent her this email to encapsulate my thoughts and hopefully give her tools for handling stress and not let it get the handle on your body or psyche.

My darling daughter,

I hope you got my voicemails. I have been praying for you and asking Jesus and His angels to cover you like a shield. Throughout life we will have forks in the road, changes in direction, setbacks and leaps. Positive change, negative change both can give us feelings of anxiety. First and foremost, know that you are not alone. You have many people that love you, especially dad and I and your brother, grandma, aunts and uncles and cousins and friends. Even in your loneliest hours, know that God, Jesus, and the Holy Spirit, the trinity, are with you. You may not see or feel His presence always; yet, like footsteps in the sand He is carrying you. There are five things that I do when I get into an anxious situation, perhaps these will help:

1. Immediately say a prayer, asking the Lord Jesus for help, out loud when possible. (Remember, when our car broke down on the way to Palm Springs? You were little and you and I said a prayer, and a tow truck showed up out of nowhere). God sends angels to help us. He gives us a way out of hard and difficult situations. Ask and you shall receive. Remember, the name of Jesus, is the most powerful name, on whom you can call anytime and He will be there for you.

2. Turn to your bible and read Psalm 91 v. 1 (911) reassures you that no pestilence, nothing can hurt you when you are covered by the lamb of God...they just pass over you...others may fall to your left or to your right, but you will remain standing...

3. Turn to your bible and read Psalm 23 "the Lord is my shepherd, no fear or want I know." I have memorized psalm 23 by heart in paraphrase, so I repeat it to myself, yes out loud when possible. Faith comes by hearing the word of God...by saying passages from the Bible out loud you strengthen and reinforce your faith with these positive affirmations.

4. No longer use the words stress, anxiety, fear, or worry. I have eliminated them from my vocabulary. Using words such as those has a spiraling affect on your psyche. Like if you keep saying I am tired, sure enough you will be more and more tired. "As a man thinks, he is". It's the same concepts you talk about as a nutritionist regarding positive body image, when you look in the mirror and tell yourself "you are beautiful". Tell yourself "I am at peace. I have a sound body

and sound mind. By His stripes I am healed". There is healing beneath his wings...all positive truths and affirmations found in the bible.

5. Make a list of all the times that God has come through for you and made the desires of your heart come to fruition. Why do you doubt then? When has he failed you? Know that he has your best interest at heart. He created you. The bible says he knitted you in the womb (think DNA strands). How can the pot look at the potter and tell it you did a lousy job? God loves you and wants you to be happy, healthy, and successful. He has given you so many talents, looks, smarts. You are just one unique amazing brand of you. Know you are special, you have purpose, and He is on your side. "Learn from the animals", says the Good Book. The birds do not worry about what they will eat, drink or wear, God presents that to them. We are His elite creation. He knows the number of hairs on our head. Wow, that's how intimately He knows us...because He made us...

I wrote a poem that I carry with me folded up in my purse to read to myself as a point of redirection when I feel like I am about to lose my peace, usually because of external influences or interactions. I have found my inner peace in Christ Jesus to whom I have relinquished all my cares; in Him I found the peace beyond understanding, the peace within the storm. As a Christian, there are still storms and many in life. Keeping our focus on Jesus, knowing that he is with us in the storm, and providing us guidance through the storm, is how I weather the storm. I know that there will be a rainbow at the end of the storm, and that "all things will be for good, for those who have faith in Jesus". I wrote this poem and I read it from time to time, as needed, to encourage myself to that peaceful point again:

Coasting Thru Life

I want to coast thru life
No worries, no strife
Just peace of mind
Living with a smile.

Coasting thru life
Celebrating day and night
Celebrating Jesus,
As He is my light.

Just coasting thru life
No worries, no strife
Knowing He is in control
Not worrying any more.

My sleep is sweet.
My mind is sound.
My body is strong.
By stress, I am not bound.

Coasting thru life with the
Wind beneath my wings.
With Jesus, I can do all things.
My spirit soars and sings.

I am coasting thru life.
No worries, no strife.
What a glorious time!
Walking with Jesus by my side.

Happiness and peace is a choice. It comes from within, not from external things or people. External forces try to steal your joy, peace and happiness, but God gave us the tools to fight the enemies and keep bad forces away. He gave us a protector and provider in Jesus our Savior. When Jesus left earth, he left us with the comforter, the power and the gifts of the Holy Spirit. So ask the Holy Spirit for strength to endure or ask Him to fight your battles. Humans are spiritual beings. Just like your body, your spirit needs food. Man cannot live by bread alone, but by the breath and words of Christ found in the Bible.

Chapter Fourteen

Another Layoff

It's 2013, and the economy is still sluggish with a GDP (Gross Domestic Product) hovering around 1 to 1.5 percent. Unemployment is around 7.5% depending on what or whose numbers you believe. Some say it may be as high as 9% as people are giving up and are no longer looking for work. Unemployment for African-American or Black American youth may be as high as 15%. The last three years, I was a fine jewelry manager. Despite the economy, people still had special occasions to celebrate like christenings, engagements, weddings, anniversaries, graduations and birthdays. The fine jewelry business was good. Diamonds and Gold were also being looked at as an alternative investment or safe haven or hedge from the falling dollar and inflation. Gold prices were soaring.

During my three years as a fine jewelry department manager, I grew and expanded the business whereby we added five cases to house more jewelry to support our fast inventory turnaround. Knowing our customers' desires, we at times sold the piece on the phone when we got it before it even went into the showcase! After all that success and growth, and achieving top sales manager two years in a row for our store, I was called in by my store manager and human resources to be told that the company no longer wanted a dedicated fine jewelry manager and that the position was being eliminated. On August 3, 2013, my position would end. My options were to take a thirteen-week severance package or look for another position within the company. I told my boss that I had anticipated this and that is why I was asking him about various positions that were becoming available in the store and that he had given to others.

When I attended the last rewards luncheon for top performers, I recognized that I was the last of the dedicated fine jewelry managers around and that most managers had other assignments in addition to fine jewelry. So his pronouncement to me did not come as a shock. What was a shock was that I was not being provided a new position. A top-performing manager of two consecutive years was being let go. Why weren't they doing musical chairs with the management responsibilities? I felt it was useless to bring up as the corporate decision was being made and human resources just executes.

My manager did tell me that a lateral position was available at another store about 45 miles south and would I be interested in interviewing? Having no other option at this time, I said I would like to interview. When I did the math computation for the gas and wear and tear on the car and the two hours daily round trip commute, the new position would be like taking a $15,000 pay cut. Again, I prayed and kept looking internally on the company jobsite for a position. Happenstance brought about that a recent new hire sales supervisor was terminated, unknown as to whether voluntary or involuntary, and the position was now open. The position would still be reduced compensation of about $8,000.

I had to now think about the quality of life. For once I decided to not put myself in the strain of taking severance and then looking for a position in this lousy labor market. Plus, my home is five minutes away from my current store and the drive and late holiday retail hours would be intense in a new location. I told my boss that I would take the sales supervisor position until a manager position became available in our store or a store preferably north, closer to my husband's workplace. By taking the sales supervisor position, I preserved more of my income, kept my short commute and received assurances that I would be considered for a management position when one opened up. At which time, my management salary would be restored was another caveat. My boss said this would be a temporary step back. I retorted out of frustration "How many times do I have to step back to finally move forward?" It was a rhetorical question, but he sensed my anguish.

I have my Bachelors in Finance, and a Masters in Organizational Development. I have been a Corporate Controller. I am a strong leader and savvy businesswoman with thirty years business experience, so why on earth should I be stepping back to get ahead? It's a mystery to me. I trust only one person and that is my Lord Jesus Christ knows the bigger picture and He has my best interest at heart. Once again I will be patient and let God's plan unfold.

Now that I took the "demotion", my ego is unsettled. The position was consolidated with fashion jewelry and accessories and given to a new college graduate, first level manager. Part of me questions why when they decided to go back to the manager owning all three accessories departments and not have a dedicated fine jewelry manager, did they not just give the two other departments to me as I was within the store prior to the new manager, seniority so to speak, doesn't count. Why revert back, and I lose out and not him. That was one question that came to mind, which I have not yet raised or brought forward. In a nutshell, they were cutting expenses heading into the fourth quarter of the year, by getting more from a newbie lower paid manager. I built the department enough with an amazing team, that it was seemingly easier to run. Demoting me was an expedient cost-cutting measure.

The other issue that I had to grapple with was that I was non-exempt salaried, and now I am exempt hourly. This is huge! I have to stop thinking beyond the clock and I have to get my work done within the clock. This one is hard for me because I am consistently thinking about my next plan of action to increase sales, to motivate associates, but I have to think differently and work more fragmented and aligned to the clock. Someone who takes ownership and wants to develop the business is thinking off the clock, that's why managers are salaried. They are paid for overall results, not by the hour.

The best time in retail is the holiday season. Our plan was to achieve total two million in annual sales. I was exhilarated at the fall season being at hand and that we would be going forward into executing our continued growth strategy. I was shooting to be top manager once again for a third year in a row. Now I am not a manager. Therefore, I am out of contention for best manager recognition. To put salt on a wound, I was expected to train and pass my knowledge to the new manager. I felt that there was age and gender inequality or flat out discrimination in how the company handled this, but I don't have the stamina to fight any longer. I was happy, however, that three members of my team achieved highest sales scores for the first week of the month of August. I left a great team of high achievers whom I was very happy to motivate and support in their achievements. My team took me out to an appreciation dinner. It was very endearing and soothing to my ego and made my spirit feel at peace.

Now that a few weeks have gone by, I am feeling at peace with my decision. I know it is temporary, and openings could come up anytime. After all the anxiety advice I had given my daughter, I subconsciously was grinding my teeth at night and having muscle and jaw discomfort during the day. Throughout the month-long endeavor of looking for positions and the uncertainty of what I would be doing or wondering if I should take severance, I was in pain. Continuing to work with a smile on my face without sharing my predicament with colleagues or subordinates was taking its toll on me. I was taking two Advil every four hours, Advil and melatonin to sleep in the evenings, and using icepacks to ease the jaw pain that was excruciating by nighttime while trying to sleep. After the word got out and I settled into the new position the pain eased. Talking with some trusted colleagues also helped my spirit to settle the pain.

I did a great deal of praying and crying in the month of July. A Christian colleague and friend of mind shared a Joel Osteen sermon with me that said "things happen for you and not to you" when you are a Christian. I needed to hear that encouragement. I tell myself and stand firm by my faith that when "Christ is with you, nothing can be against you". I firmly believe that "all things come to good for those who have faith in Christ". Still, we are human and we are frail and faith comes by hearing the word. Having Christian friends who support you through these events is a great blessing.

It was hard to explain to my young adult son why and how it is that when someone is the top manager in the store two consecutive years in a row that a company would decide to indiscriminately lay them off or demote them as a preferred action. He too was perplexed and basically came to the conclusion which is fostered in the public school system that working hard doesn't pay off or matter. In his high school graduation year, I said to him hope you will get the high grades so you can walk with a gold robe. His sister and two cousins graduated from his school with gold robes. He responded to me that they do not do that anymore, because everyone is the same and they don't want the people with lower grades to feel inferior or bad. So the incentives for working hard are removed and there is no recognition. This event at work reinforced his skewed liberal public high school brain washing. It also made me rethink why I work so hard and take pride and ownership in my work. I have to continuously remind myself that I am working to serve a higher purpose, my Almighty God. I continue to walk by faith and not by sight. Amen.

The reduction in pay, and hourly wages rather than salary, made it financially difficult to continue being effective when financial demands continues. With two young adults in college, and no certainty as to when a management position would materialize in the store, I continued to be assertive in looking for internal management positions. Finally, I found and applied for a position about forty-five miles north at the Mission Viejo Macy's store. The interview went really well and I accepted the position. The exact day after I accepted the position, the young man in the executive training program whose position as Handbag and Fashion Jewelry manager was expanded to Center Core manager, with the addition of the Fine Jewelry department into his areas of responsibility, decided to return to his home state where he will be married. With a great deal of back and forth discussion as to the inopportune timing and what do I really want, I decided to honor my new position and keep it so as to broaden my horizons with the anticipation of one day being a Vice-President Store Manager. I started in the new store on October 15 and quickly commenced to escalate the team plus seasonal hires towards the holiday shopping season.

The organizational culture in the new store is very different than that of my other store. That is perhaps the greatest lesson learned. Every Macy store will have its own culture. The culture is defined by store history, management, personnel and the customers. My positive personality and tolerance of diversity seems to play a great function in the reason I am hired into a position. As a repeat of history (Read my book called "But She's Not a Guy), I am being hired into a new green team in fine jewelry, with a top producer on Leave of Absence, and a history where the old team voluntarily disbanded for a variety of unknown or rumored reasons. To the point, where I found that some of the team-members who were now in other departments refused to work or want back into the department.

In the handbags and fashion jewelry department, I discovered a team that was not synergistic, perhaps antagonistic, visibly at times in front of customers. Immediately on my arrival, a lead tenured, full time top producer retires right before black Friday and the holiday season. The company decides not to fill her position with a permanent person, but seasonal hires. So going into the holiday season literally set up for failure, so each associate and the largely seasonal team were critical to making sales goals. Training all the new seasonal hires especially in fine jewelry was tantamount and difficult. We made it through the holidays without completely addressing behavioral or cultural teamwork issues aspiring to do so once the holidays subsided.

The serendipity of all that occurred in late 2013 was that at the same time that I was given a layoff notice, my sister was also given a pink slip from her employer of thirty years. She too was scurrying to find an internal position within her high-tech employer. The day I began my job was the same day she began her new job. So we both were going through the same ordeal. In this case, misery does not like company as she had not really experienced this before, whereas, this was probably my fourth experience with job change due to mergers, acquisitions, layoffs, a trail of experiences that I have had the grievous pleasure to endure. She had great anxiety over the potential loss of income with two young adults in college as well.

Even with the start of a new job, as I near age 55, I toy with the idea of how and when would I be able to retire. Retirement seems further and further away as my income rolls back rather than lunging forward, while cost of living and taxes go up and education loans for both myself and my husband and the parent PLUS loans for my daughter are all coming due. Retirement is a bleak picture for now. I try not to think about it too often as I still have my son in college and living at home. He has at least two more years to go, perhaps even three, as courses aren't always available to take. He is financially astute. He wants to live at home while going to college so as to not incur debt. He is working and paying his own gas, lunches and entertainment. My husband and I are very proud of him. He is focused on his education, his work and his music. He is smart and very talented, more grounded and mellow than his parents. We are also very proud of our daughter who is on her way to being a Registered Dietician. She too is smart, beautiful and talented. Both took after their father in their understanding of the sciences, their love for music and performance. From me, my daughter took my assertive and analytical traits and my son took my philosophical and introspective nature.

Being the sandwich generation, our lives seem to be in a continuous holding pattern. We don't know what shoe is going to drop next with our children, our parents, ourselves, our work, and how we will be able to respond to life's demands. I believe I have a good support system with a husband, a sister and a mom who loves me. As our lives go forward, each individual has their own issues that they are struggling with and trying to resolve, but we are all still somehow there for one another as best we can in various instances in our lives. At times, it becomes too overwhelming and that is when I know to turn to a higher power, Jesus Christ, for His infinite and saving grace, mercy and favor!

Fell In Love

I fell in love at eighteen.
Didn't know it would last.
Never thought it wouldn't.
Time just passed.

With every twist and turn,
Loving you even deeper,
So many changes happened
Yet out love grew sweeter.

With a lovely daughter
And a handsome son
A house, a dog,
And unending fun,

You think we would get older
And perhaps even bored.
Yet when you look at me
My spirit still soars!

Chapter Fifteen

How on Earth to Retire

My husband and I decided to take a mini vacation to Avila Beach in California and really enjoyed our time together. We went to the famous Madonna Inn for breakfast and the various shops at Morro Bay and walked around the college town San Luis Obispo, and visited its beautiful Mission. We bought crab from the fishermen at the pier and a bottle of wine from Trader Joe's and just enjoyed our time together on the beach. This perhaps is the feeling or retirement or maybe not.

During our vacation, we met another couple and just started a conversation. They shared their excitement about how they were on a cross-country trip together in their RV. They didn't seem much older than us, perhaps plus or minus five years. They said that they decided to "Sell Everything" purchased an RV and hit the road to wherever it took them. No responsibilities, no mail, just the open road ahead. I shuddered at the thought of sleeping in an RV day in day out and not having roots, neighbors, family, etc. They are braver than me. I also shuddered at the gas that an RV took at now nearing four dollars per gallon. I don't know how far your money can take you with your retirement nest egg burning as fuel.

Some time ago, my husband and I took a weekend cruise to Ensenada, Mexico and back to California. On that cruise, I met an elderly woman who decided that she wanted to be catered to, not in an old age home, rather on cruise ships! In her retirement, she travels the world on continuous cruises. She said it's basically like an all inclusive retirement home, but she is traveling, meeting new people and new places all the time and has great meals, entertainment and a doctor on board. No roots, just literally cruising through life. This sounds like an awesome idea for those who have no roots and no fruit. I want and anticipate grandchildren and great grandchildren and want to enjoy them at times while cognizant.

My dad worked in his own business until he couldn't get out of bed anymore with his COPD. He died at age 82. My mom worked so that they would have health insurance coverage for the family and a steady income to subsidize my father's entrepreneurial spirit. She retired as soon as my dad was 65 and covered by Medicare. She was 55 at her retirement. They had worked and saved consistently in laddered CDs and insured municipal bonds with a secure rate of return. Their home was practically paid off with a very small monthly mortgage payment. Even in retirement, they were able to provide gifts to their grandchildren and assistance to their children during hard economic times. It's amazing how they did it!

The challenge is, once the kids are grown and on their path, how to simplify life and create a manageable enjoyable lifestyle on a fixed income. Deciding what is a priority and being of same mind with your spouse is also a challenge. The formula seems simple enough. You either raise your income or raise your savings, and reduce your expenses. As a financial planner, I have found that people that make millions can also easily spend millions. There are also people who make less than $50,000, who live frugally and maximize their savings and make sound investments. In the end, they have no debt, a nice retirement cushion, which allows them to sleep comfortably and securely each night. Their saved money, earns the money they need to live from, and the principle is their inheritance to their children or grandchildren.

The sandwich generation is fearful that their parents will spend their inheritance on healthcare or long-term care as generations are living longer. Also, their children can't seem to graduate from school, they are incurring lots of student loans and can't seem to locate good paying jobs when they graduate. It looks like the sandwich generation is getting eaten alive from both ends. The veteran generation had company pension plans that provided nice annuities alongside social security for their retirement. Some lucky baby boomers had pension plans, particularly if they were union or government employees. Today's generation X is dependent on 401k plans attached to an uncertain and volatile stock market in a volatile world. Gen Y's are still in college and living at home again with parents, just pitiful and scary!

I am now 55 and my husband 58. He works in private education, and feels forever young. I work in retail and feel sometimes young, sometimes very old. In spirit, I am young, in body not so much. My husband exercises more than I. I know that I need to exercise also, but I am wiped out from being on my feet all day or night in retail. Walking my dog is my exercise, but I need more cardio and weight loss. I try to get that in on my days off. On working days, I come home exhausted, physically and mentally fatigued!

I have also met couples that decide to forgo the American lifestyle and take their savings and social security direct deposits to live in a foreign country like Greece, Istanbul, Mexico, Ecuador, or Armenia. Live in a location where their US dollars are valuable and the cost of living is low, and they can retire like kings. We came from a foreign land to live the American dream and have opportunity. I don't mind visiting other countries, or even extended stays, but not as a home. My home is America and I like it that way. I want to be close to my children and eventual grandchildren. Although both my children feel, at this point, that the world has run amuck and they don't want to bring children into this world. They see the sacrifices we are making for their success and they are not ready to make those sacrifices now at age 26 and 21. I believe and hope that this is a phase. I try to show the other side of how bland my life would be without them and that they are my joy! At some point in a relationship you want to procreate out of the love for each other and the amazing grace, blessings and sheer love and joy that a child brings to bond your union and families. Parenting is a phenomenal stage of life that cannot be fully fathomed or understood until you have held your child in your arms and gone through the anticipation and awe of that moment! That unconditional love is out of this world and fulfills the spiritual endeavor of the circle of life. It's pure innocent agape love!

How to retire is a growing challenge. Selling the house seems an easy way out, but the hope was to leave something to our children of value so they don't have to struggle as much as we did. The potential of owning a home seems more and more out of reach at this time as young people further their education and it takes average six years to get a bachelors degree. Not to mention $100,000 or more in student loan debt. With job scarcity and the inability of young people to form households, the natural thing is to continue in academia with a masters and additional student loans. So graduating with looming debt over them, a shorter work life and a potentially longer lifespan, it's a huge quandary for the millennial. The sandwich generation is carrying everyone's burdens and we need creative out-of-the box solutions.

We live in a beachside tourist community. One of our thoughts was to rent our furnished homes out as vacation rentals and live as renters wherever life takes us in retirement. It sounds awesome to me and I am ready to execute that plan today! My son has two more years in college to complete, and as soon as he does this may be just the plan. Vacation home rentals can be quite lucrative if rented year-round, which our area does have year-round tourism. Vacation home rental is definitely a strong possible road to retirement. I like the option because we don't have to sell everything in order to make it happen. In the event that it isn't rented we could move back in and use either home. We also have a couple of timeshares, so we may be able to experience various living situations as needed to optimize income. These are times for desperate measures. Our 401k is depleted due to recessions, layoffs, underemployment, flat line incomes, and inflation particularly in energy, education and healthcare costs. Pension plans are being ceased by many major companies opting for defined contribution 401k plans, rather than, defined benefit annuity plans.

We have toyed with how to maximize our 401k contributions. I chose to convert to a ROTH IRA as my income is so low now and my housing, itemized deductions are so high that I would rather pay the lower taxes now than to pay taxes later. My husband's plan matches so much more than my employer, that it behooves us to maximize his contributions. The fallacy of catch-up contributions is if you didn't save in your early years, that you now have more money to invest into yourself. This is so far from being true at this point, that it's laughable. My prime working years were 21 through 30. People need to start saving the day that they start earning money, due to the luxury of time and compounding interest. Your thirties and forties are your prime spending years, building the nest, populating it and teaching your fledglings to fly.

Often, there are no discretionary monies to save or splurge with unless you watch your dollars very carefully. You can make more and save nothing or make less and save more of it. Rarely do you find people who make more and save more. You want to invest and have a return on your investment. You want to work and then you want your money to work for you. You goal yourself to where when you don't want to work, or are unable to work, you have a nest egg that is producing a monthly income for you to live from. You must know that life has pitfalls due to health, finances, unemployment, family circumstances that veer us away from saving and can cause us to deplete our resources. So we must have the insurances and safety nets to meet those life's challenges.

Retirement is something I can taste each time we go on vacation, yet seems far into the distance. In your youth, you relish the concept and actualization of your first job, first car, owning a home, and first promotion. You get sucked into the hype and materialism of the brand name logo sneakers, sunglasses, clothes, handbags, cars and lifestyles. So you flick away all your hard earned money into the wind and you have to work harder and harder to keep those relished feelings. The excitement starts fading and you are working harder to satiate something lacking with more and more materialism.

My friend, my reader, the most gratifying things are those that are free. Stop and enjoy life and people around you. Put down the electronics and try having a day without money and things. It's a huge challenge at first. But you used to do it in your youth, in the playground, a family picnic or at the beach. Look into the eyes of your loved ones - spouse, parents, children, or friends. Sit beside them, hug them, lean on each other, hold hands, have a conversation about feelings, desires of the heart, goals, fears, and plans.   Play with your dog. Watch birds and butterflies while tending to the flowers, vegetables, fruits and herbs from your own garden. Go for a walk and say hello to neighbors.

The Rhino

So strong, so invincible,

Yet nearing extinction.

Focused and head strong

Yet so vulnerable.

Tough impenetrable exterior

Yet so fragile.

You are alive now,

Yet extinct in an instant.

Chapter Sixteen

Reinvention

How many times does one have to reinvent themselves? "When the going gets tough, the tough get going!" You have to pull yourself up by the bootstraps, and get up on that horse and ride again! Or, get another horse that will take you to where you want to go! The answer to the question, is you will have to reinvent yourself as often as needed. Either as often as circumstances require you to change, or as often as you wish to drive change in your own life. We are in an era of continuous learning and growth. The choice is yours to learn, be current, significant and grow, or be stagnant and obsolete.

Thus far in my life, I have worked in corporate accounting and finance, personal finance, equities and insurance sales, computers and peripheral technology controller, construction controller, recruiter, beauty advisor, cosmetic counter manager, fine jewelry manager, retail sales manager, and now once again I am pulling at my bootstraps to find which horse to ride this time! I have worked for a fortune 500 company, a Venture Capital financed mid-size company, a small family owned business, had my own accounting services business, had my own financial planning practice and insurance agency, plus a consulting business. How is it that I find myself in this predicament once again?

Part of me says start your own business once again as an author, speaker, and consultant. Another part of me says, you still have so many expenses and responsibilities for your son and daughter's education, potential wedding costs perhaps, until they are both settled you need a steady income with benefits. So this time around, I am looking at an industry that continuously exists and is growing of necessity as people are living longer. The industry I am aspiring to join is the pharmaceutical sales industry. So I am studying to get the certification.

The irony of this situation is while I am studying the pharmaceutical sales industry, my husband, who is a biochemist, is going for his MBA and taking Management courses. It's like we are playing in each other's sandboxes, but we are also helping each other with terms and concepts.

Continuous learning has become a way of life. If you don't continuously learn and grow, you will wither and die or become extinct. The world has been, always was and forever will be in a continuous state of change or evolution. A person has to evolve with the world or create their own world with their own paradigms and values. Either path requires energy, resilience, flexibility, plus a positive, optimistic attitude that embraces change.

Look at the world around you. Development is moving at a faster pace. New products used to come to market every five to ten years. That sped up to new developments in three to five years. More recently, it's six to eighteen months! No sooner than you have purchased the most recent gadget or upgrade, the industry launches a new device or new features.

Everyday a new medical study is announced about what we eat and drink. We are inundated with claims of "new and improved", "fat free", "gluten free", "no trans fat", "no sugar", "no high fructose corn syrup", "hormone free", "organic", "cage-free", etc. Even the cows and chickens are confused! There are so many supplements and holistic, herbal drugs for practically every ailment, along with all the over the counter or prescription drugs that are out there with various benefits, side effects, and complications. Once again the consumer or patient is in a quandary as to what to take and whose recommendations to trust. On line self-diagnosis sites, urgent care facilities, easy-access pharmacy retail clinics, their primary care physician and often the physician's assistant or nurse practitioner all provide various levels of care and advice. Whose advice to heed?

In retail, every weekend claims sales, discounts, clearance or lowest prices, with or without coupons, to the point where you have to be a math whiz to calculate as to when it is to your advantage to purchase. Consumers have so many ways now to access and find what they want. We are in the age of the informed consumer. The individual who researches and compares features, benefits, prices, financing, shipping charges, taxes, guarantees and warranties. Even after their purchase, they are on the lookout for the better price to get their price adjustment, to get the companies to match prices to gain or retain their sale. They can buy online, deliver items to their home or nearest store. It's quite a conundrum of choices available at your fingertips!

Everyone is reinventing themselves. Yes, the whole world is reinventing themselves. Look at the growth and advancement in the labor force and economic benefits reaped in Japan, China, Korea, and India as the United States of America transitioned from manufacturer of goods to a nation of research and development and intellectual properties. For those who didn't change, learn or attain new skills at the pace of the changing economic wave in these foreign countries, fell into the infamous economic skill gap. This skill gap exists today. The jobs that are available and in demand do not have the appropriate labor force with the skills in science, math, engineering, technology to fill them. People are in shock! How did we fall into this pit called "the skill gap" and how on earth do we as a nation, a company, or an individual climb out of it? Particularly hard hit are the baby boomers who have been working some 10, 20, 30 years with one employer or in one industry or trade. Now, as an example, it's been automated and they need to know CAD/CAM. In some cases it's less expensive and more cost-effective in dollars, time, and efficiencies to hire a new younger trained individual than, forgive the phrase, "to teach an old dog new tricks."

Take myself for example, at age 56, I feel like I am 36. The working world wants to call me and treat me as 56. What gives my age away is my depth of knowledge and experience, perhaps the crow feet or slight sag in the brows or cheek line. As I gaze in the magnifying mirror I am perplexed, as I try to reaffirm and encourage myself that "for 56 you look hot!" Then I look closer and wonder if Botox is necessary.

One of my favorite books is "Who moved my cheese?" by Spencer Johnson. Most often, we know things are amiss or change is happening, but we are in denial, or can't seem to put the pieces together to be able to see the inevitable writing on the wall! Often, we feel stuck between a rock and a hard place and don't know what actions to take. Or, we know what we need to do, but we procrastinate, primarily due to fear. So, we have to break the chains that bind us often in our own minds and have confidence, have no fear and take the first step of courage towards a new path. When staying stuck and becoming extinct is the other option, then fear has no grip, rather a leap of faith is warranted.

The leap of faith I am speaking of is where "reinvention" begins. How do we do things differently, seamlessly, faster, easier, or better? What resources do we need? What education or training do we need? How do we focus on what is important, our core strengths, core values, our customers and clients. Reinvention at times can take the form of an evolution or at times it is painstaking in the form of a revolution. For an employee, the leap of faith may be in the form of a new company, a new job within the same company, a whole new industry, or an entrepreneurial endeavor like opening your own business. It takes a leap of faith to reinvent oneself. The greatest faith is in yourself, your talents, your energy, your wisdom and faith in a higher source to guide you, to strengthen you to help you persist and persevere. One has to muster a determination and affirmation in faith and optimism that things and circumstances will get better.

How long will reinvention take and how do we persist in the meantime? This is where short term and long term perspectives and goals have to be assessed. If you live only for short-term gains and profits, the long-term issues will catch up with you with a rude reawakening! For example, for years America did not invest in infrastructure, such as roads, bridges, pipelines, dams, transportation and our cities and the people within felt this gap. Look at Hurricane Katrina as one huge, painful example when the levies broke and flooded Louisiana and rendered thousands of people in New Orleans homeless and displaced.

Then again, you can plan for the long-term, but cannot lose sight of current or short term needs, such as food on the table, gas in your car, or the utilities bill. Sometimes, one gets mired in current pressing issues of addiction, illness, drowning in debt, grief, and depression. Sometimes, we don't know a way out of this maze. It's easier to give up than to muster up the energy to move forward and even to get out of bed. This is when we have to look to a higher power. We have to reach out to assistance and talk. It could be a family member, a doctor, a therapist, a priest, an anonymous hotline, an employee assistance program through work, a councilor at school, or a friend. It is good to talk to someone. Even go to the beach find a private spot and yell it out to the heavens and talk to a higher power! You can listen, but always consider the source of the advice, still weigh it and reaffirm it with other credible sources before making a decision. Leap of faith can also be called a calculated risk; it doesn't have to be totally blind! Research and be resourceful to know your options, so you can make an informed choice.

Today I was let go, discharged, from work. Did I see it coming? Yes. It became very clear to me when my boss asked me to step into his office and put me on a performance improvement plan (PIP) a couple of months ago because my team was not making sales plan. My team was fairly new and I was training them, but there is a long training curve for fine jewelry. It takes knowledge and finesse to romance the stone and develop an emotional sale. Although, other managers were not making sales goal or credit goal, they were not targeted for PIP. My deep intuition is that the company needed to make fourth quarter numbers. Due to my salary being higher than a new college graduate's salary, it is a cost cutting measure to let me go. October is the time for the layoffs, so companies squeeze a profit for the quarter and scramble to make the year's financial plan.

Was I prepped for it? Yes, financially to a limited degree. I curtailed various expenses, and saved a little money. Much more prepared than the last time it happened with the 2008 bank and real estate collapse. From the last lay off, I had already refinanced my first home, now a rental, and my current residence to a fixed rate mortgage with a lower interest rate. I already had cut cable to basic, and paid off my car. Threw garage sales and sold a bunch of extra things like furniture, clothes, and toys.

Was I taking action in preparation for it? Yes, I was studying for a certification in a new career in pharmaceutical sales. Even tested for the certification once but got 75%, when I needed 80% to pass. Again, I will get on that horse and try once more to pass. I wanted to do something in sales, but something more challenging, more service to society, and with better compensation than the sales manager position in retail industry. I see this change as a positive change to my next great opportunity. It is time to re-coop the losses of this last seven years. I feel we lived through the seven lean years and now it's time to enjoy the glorious years of abundance! It's time to be the pitcher, not just the cup! Through the trial, you gain perseverance, courage, discipline, patience, and confidence. From the sacrifice and the suffering comes the launch to glory!

Was I emotionally ready for it? No, it hurts. I miss my colleagues. I miss my direct reports. I miss getting up and getting ready for work each day. I don't like the question from acquaintances or neighbors of how is work going? It's not! I am looking for the next great thing the Lord commissions me to do. I know whatever it is; it will be awesome and amazing!

On the bright side, I don't have to deal with black-Friday sales this year that are starting as early as six o'clock on Thanksgiving Day! Managers and some associates come an hour earlier at five, and basically Thanksgiving Day and dinner with the family is shot. My daughter is coming home from Boston for Thanksgiving and I will get to enjoy being with her. I am very excited about celebrating the holidays with my family. I don't have to work or commute the hour to work on late nights or early mornings for retail holiday hours! God gave me peace for this holiday season and time to breathe and enjoy my turkey, eggnog, and pumpkin pie! So Reinvention, here I go again!

With arduous study and taking and retaking the quizzes, I passed the test and obtained the Certified Pharmaceutical Sales Representative (CPNR) certification. I quickly updated my resume and applied to various pharmaceutical representative positions. As quickly as I applied, I received responses stating, "We have determined not to pursue your application further". Ugly! As I was speaking with my daughter, she informed me that she knew two individuals that were in the pharmaceutical sales industry. One a beautiful smart young friend of hers and another friend's mother, both of whom became disgruntled with the industry as they felt pressured to be taking doctors to lunches and "schmoozing" doctors for their prescription business. That seems so contrary to the pharmaceutical study that I just completed regarding having clinical trial discussions and keeping doctors abreast of newest studies regarding the medications or competitors medications, formularies, disease indications, etc. My daughter's and her primary sources felt that the industry is for young assertive gregarious females to attract resident and older doctors to prescribe. At this time, I am going to give the industry the benefit of the doubt and uncover the realities myself. I filed for unemployment, plus I rented a room in my home, and cut expenses (cable, landscaper, dining out, gas, insurance) so I have a year in which to find an appropriate position and redirection.

I also have under consideration my books, speaking engagements, and business consulting. I once shared with a realtor friend "we are waiting for our ships to come in" about some of the endeavors my husband and I are trying to accomplish. She intuitively responded, "It's good you have sent ships out!" I thought that is so correct, we, as a family, have worked hard to create or "reinvent" our selves individually. Time will tell which path will unfold and be more fruitful.

Why Am I Here?

Look down on the ground
See the ants scurry.
Look up at the blue sky
See the birds fly.
Look into our Milky- way
See the swirl of stars.

Look into your hands
And ask what can I do?
Then do it!

Seek to do acts of kindness,
To draw a smile or a laugh
To give what others lack
And pass it forward or give back.
Use your hands to love and comfort
To create and cut needs to half.

Hear the crashing waves,
And the chirping crickets
In the still of the night.
Look at your feet
And ask where should I be?
Then go there!

Seek to spread peace and joy
Listen to help and advise
Go to make a difference
Invent solutions
Achieve results.

Be courageous in adversity.
Be patient in trials.
Forgive your enemies.
Speak truth and inspire

Be thankful for gifts of grace.
Love yourself and your neighbor.
And above all love God
As you are here to go, do, seek and speak His Word.

Chapter Seventeen

Age Discrimination

Is it or isn't it age discrimination? In lay terms it is. In legal ease it isn't. Let me share a few scenarios: The company decides that managers will utilize an IPad within the store. Rather than purchase one per manager, the company wants the management team to share one IPad loaded with various coaching, customer feedback and flash software. A store manager receives the new business toy and asks at the management meeting who would like to be the first to try it for the day. Six managers, from one month to 15 years of experience, in the room remain silent. The manager with the most expertise breaks the silence and says "I will take it, I love trying new technology." The store manager says out loud to everyone looking around the room "I wanted someone more technologically savvy to be the first to use it." To which the senior manager responded, while reaching for the IPad in the store manager's hand, "I believe I am fairly savvy to using technology!" How do you see this scenario? How do you think the various individuals felt about this at the daily management meeting? Who was most sensitive or least sensitive to this scenario and in what nuance?

How about this next scenario: An experienced manager is having a regular weekly coaching meeting with their superior. The superior says I have asked the human resources manager to join in this week's coaching session. As part of the session, the superior pulls out a Performance Improvement Plan form, and requests that the seasoned manager complete a response as to how they are going to bring their business back on plan. After the meeting the human resource manager, discreetly says to the manager perhaps they should consider stepping to a less stressful position. "Think of a time when you were happiest? She recommends. "I am extremely happy now. I love my job, my people, and my customers." Says I, a seasoned manager, wondering what the f___ is happening?

Is everyone who is below various benchmarks being put on PIP, within the store, within other stores? One asks that question, but is told that is of no consequence to them, they need to consider only their own performance. "Is that for real?" What if the seasoned manager was several time an award winner recognized for highest scorecard, best manager, best sales, best credit performance…How does this scenario fit in with age discrimination? How would other managers feel when they discover this is happening with one of their colleagues within the store? How would others in previous stores where the manager worked, colleagues and subordinates, feel about how the manager is being treated?

Here's a third scenario: In one of these coaching sessions the manager says to an experienced, awarded manager: "It's not your dedication, enthusiasm or your hard work that I am questioning, it is your ability." How would you feel if you were this seasoned, awarded, educated manager with a Bachelors and a Masters in Business, who shows up to work each day with enthusiasm, dedication and service-orientation. Are we yet able to call this age discrimination?

How about if these scenarios all happened to one individual along with other soft scenarios? As a layperson you may think that it smells like, sounds like, feels like, looks like age discrimination, let's call it as it is. But, try to prove it in a case of law. If there is any business reason for the above behavior, the employee endures it until it escalates and they are fired, or they are forced to resign. How pitiful is all this? This is why it is so important if one works for a company to be ready and prepped at a drop of a hat to be ready to leave, financially, educationally, emotionally always have a plan B. Always, have an alternate source of income. Particularly, have a source of passive income that doesn't always take your continuous physical effort. Income sources on which you can rely on such as rental income from investment properties, stock dividends, or interest from corporate or municipal bonds or leverage oneself with employees in your own business, or from a side home-based business that can grow with low inventories or low overhead.

Always be prepared for the lean years with savings or interest income, dividends income from investments. If these extra funds aren't used in lean years, then they will be a source for your retirement that comes much earlier that you expected. Remember those first fine lines around your eyes, how they appeared one morning in the mirror? That's how age and retirement creeps up on us where the mind maybe willing but the body is not, or vice a versa. Sometimes, work curtailment is forced upon us through illness or disability or even due to circumstances of caring for you aging or disabled parents, spouse or God forbid, children. Perhaps you even chose retirement as a time to do a second career that you have always imagined that you will do in the future when all the stars and universe are in alignment. Sometimes, companies advise you to go into retirement or to resign to make room for more current employees either with education, looks, social network, energy, personality, and optimism! Start aligning the stars and planets today, at least those that are within your grasp in the event something not in your control transpires.

To the managers and companies that use some of those soft, yet unscrupulous tactics to eliminate their less desirable employees, remember that you reap what you sow. Older employees that perhaps did not keep up, were not trained, who did not want to relocate, train to take on more or newer responsibilities, should be let go with an early retirement package or golden parachute, not put through the "soft separation" torture techniques. Let's be honest and offer a no-fault ticket for separation as is commonly done with CEO's. If it's good for the goose, then why is it not good for the gander? Then age discrimination would not be such an issue. We are not stupid. Ok, so you want younger, sexier, less expensive, more tech savvy, new breeds, just say so, and pay me to leave, don't kick me in the gut and tell me that I am unable to do my work! Pay the unwanted elders a fair separation severance without the agony of degradation.

So, do I pick myself up and dust myself off and go back into the working world once again with a smile on my face? Do I stay hopeful that there is a good, decent, fair valued company out there and I will not get beat up again? If you have read my prior books, over thirty years of employment, I survived three layoffs; endured a forced resignation for having a child which wasn't in my employer's plan, and now this forced discharge due to what I think is fourth quarter cost reduction, they say is performance (BS).

I am 56, feel like 36, and look like 46 and uncertain whether I want to endure the interview process from some of these companies. In order to keep my resume under the two pages, I had to delete half my working life. As a working mother with childcare issues, exiting the work force and reentering at a lower paying job makes my resume fragmented. As a member of the sandwich generation, adult care issues like caring for aging in-laws, parents, childless aunts and uncles, also pull you out of a straight up arrow career path. It's really tiring to have to explain your life's twists and turns and zigzags to potential recruiters, human resource personnel and hiring managers.

So what is a job applicant to do to defy age discrimination? There are so many thoughts on the resume: not chronological, list only those jobs relevant to the job you are applying for, create a skills resume and sort jobs to support the skills, don't put any dates, exclude some jobs, the list goes on and on. How does one present themselves and what they are capable of accomplishing reflected on two pages? How does one take a lifetime of work and experiences and abridge it to two 8 1/2 x 11 sheets of paper? It is very challenging to show who you are on two pieces of paper, when half your life no longer counts.

I had my own business when my son was asthmatic as a child, along with a part-time job to keep the health benefits and while simultaneously going to school to get my Masters in Organizational Management. Once again, this may be another perfect time to provide my services to other businesses and entrepreneurs. Finally, focus on being what I always wanted to be a speaker, author, consultant, business advisor similar to Ken Blanchard and John Maxwell. Companies don't have to be ruthless and cut throat to be successful. They can artfully and compassionately manage relationships and expectations with all their stakeholders. Happy employees, vendors, customers, investors all blend and overflow into a productive profitable day, month, year, and decades of servicing others. A life full of service to others is a life fulfilled.

It comes back to why are we here? Are we fulfilling our purpose for which we were created and born? For me, the question daily persists "How can I fulfill the will of God in my life?" I do believe that things don't happen to me, they happen for me. Sometimes, I have been resistant to move on, even when the writing is on the wall, out of fear and anxiety. I have to remind myself, the greatest fear is the taking of that first step. Once you take the first step, the next step will naturally follow and the momentum continues. Sometimes, we have to take a deep breath, say a little prayer and lunge forward. Sometimes, over analysis, like writing the business plan over three times, may be wasting precious market time or missing the window of opportunity. We need to learn to take those calculated risks, build the confidence we need to do so with education, research and development, competitive analysis, so that we can take that step forward.

As a Christian, we "walk by faith and not by sight", knowing full well that "He is the lamp upon my feet, and the light onto my path." Trust your gut or intuition, have faith in God and His divine purpose for your life and move forward with self-confidence. The Good Book says success comes from the combination of confidence, courage, perseverance and patience. Through the struggle come the confidence and the glory. The courage, perseverance or steadfastness and the patience are gifts from the Holy Spirit, so those come from the spirit.

Before Christ died on the cross, He told the apostles that when he is gone, they are to gather together and he is going to send a comforter. When Christ died, the apostles were scared where Peter denied Him and Thomas doubted Him. It wasn't until after the Holy Spirit came upon them, on the day of Pentecost, that they started talking in tongues and some spoke and some understood other languages that they suddenly had the courage to go out into the world and be disciples proclaiming Christ's teachings and miracles on earth and promise of eternal life. This is the spirit, the light of fire placed within us, which we need to tap into to achieve real and lasting success in our purpose.

The beauty, magic, power, secret or whatever you want to call this amazing grace, is that it is available to us free for asking for it. So ask the Lord Jesus Christ for His forgiveness, guidance, mercy, and grace and ask the Holy Spirit for courage, peace, patience, fortitude and self-control. I particularly pray to the Holy Spirit to give me self-control over my thoughts and my words. As a man thinks he is, and as you speak will come to pass. There is great power in the thought and then in the spoken word. Not every thought needs to be uttered or given to realization. Self-control is the gift of controlling those two powerful entities: your thoughts and your words. If one controls their thoughts and their words, then taking first actionable step doesn't seem as daunting. That first step of courage is brought down to a manageable first step, not an obstacle of a mountain to climb.

Chapter Eighteen

Barriers to Entry

Speaking of mountains, the barriers that are either real or artificial in our minds can be found everywhere. These barriers are inherent in everyone, especially when one individual or their environment or situation is different from the others. The barriers are more evident or transparent depending on the sensitivities and the backgrounds of the participants. When I was growing up, my parents moved, from the Middle East to America, to provide their two daughters opportunities that did not exist in Middle-Eastern countries. My parents taught us that the sky is the limit and you can achieve anything you want under the sun, especially in America.

Nobody spoke of the glass ceiling, or unequal pay or discrimination. No one spoke of limitations inherent or not in the color of your hair, color of your eyes, color of your skin, your gender, your religion, your sexual persuasion, your weight, your accent, what you ate, the type of car you drive, which school you graduated from. Discerning differences is an inherent part of life and being. People have preferences based on their experiences, their expectations, their knowledge and backgrounds. The issue comes in when discrimination is used or acted upon to the detriment of others. People are biased. A mother may think her child is the prettiest, handsomest, smartest, or most talented in the room. The reality is they may very well be, or they may not be, so how is the mother or the child going to go about their daily business and interactions with other children, teachers, or parents. When do preferences become discriminatory and harmful to others and when does it create a barrier to their success, or inhibit their growth, sustainability or limit opportunity.

We all know of the stories of the horrors of the genocide that Armenian people endured and survived in 1915. We all know the stories of the horrors of the holocaust that Jewish people endured and survived in 1940. We all know of the horrors of the Rwandan massacres in 1994. More recently, who can forget the gassing of the people in Syria and the persecution of Christians and moderate Muslims throughout the world by Islamic terrorists as ISIS? Discrimination or crimes of hate are real and have been around from the beginning of Biblical times since Cain and Able, an individual killing his own brother.

As a member of the sandwich generation, we are passing on our likes, dislikes, fears and discriminatory thoughts to our children, knowingly or unknowingly. We may also be discarding some of those discriminatory thoughts that our parents may have passed on us. At the same time, our children are going off to college and expanding their horizons and sometimes coming home with thoughts positive and negative that is new to us. So what elements in society, given today's age of technology, seemingly open borders, college loans, philanthropic or social aid is still creating barriers to entry, growth and prosperity.

Much of the barriers are in our heads. Real or unreal, an individual has to seek out ways to overcome the barriers. Some say they lack the money, the time, the energy, or the mobility. They look at their own conception of barriers in the mirror and succumb to those self-defeating thoughts. Others look at the barriers and say I am going to utilize them for good, for achievement, for helping others, for making a change, for speaking out so others don't get persecuted. So people choose to convert the barriers to entry into bridges to entry! Here rather than seeing their own differences as lack, they see and discern that everyone is different in some ways, but similar in other, perhaps more important ways. As the Reverend Martin Luther King said, "Judge a person not by the color of their skin, but the content of their character." I would also say that "Judge not what they say or look like, but what they actually do or have done." Politicians are quick to say as Hillary Clinton said when testifying in the Congressional Hearing on Benghazi, where we lost a US Ambassador and three other brave Embassy Personnel, "What does it matter, how they lost their lives?" The Executive Branch had concocted a story about riots over a movie, versus what everyone else in Intelligence was calling a terrorist attack. This made up story was to ward off negative imagery and withhold the truth of why the Embassy was attacked and four Americans killed, to smooth the way for President Obama's second term reelection. The lie also reinforced the smoke screen that Al Qaeda was dismantled post Osama's execution, avenging the 9/11/2001 attack that killed 4000 people in the New York World Trade Center Twin Towers.

In the end, the barriers to entry, the various forms of discrimination that people endure, can be viewed as bridges to a better world or society. Our responses to these crimes of hate are what shape our future. Do we show compassion, forgiveness, or do we retaliate with more hate that fuels the fire further? The recent attacks in Boston during the marathon, and the one in Paris at the edgy cartoon magazine come to mind. In both cases, we had fatalities due to hatred, but we also had survivors who dug deep and overcame and showed solidarity with passionate movements as "Boston Strong" and "Je Sui Charlie". Once again, out of the struggle came strength, confidence and glory.

So back to earth, my dear patient reader, my soul is in a struggle. I am a woman at age 56 feeling the barriers to entry. At 56, my mother was already retired. I got married later, had my children later, so I still have one child in college. The college students who can't find jobs are still either continuing in school or working lower level hourly wage jobs and moving back in with their parents. My son lives with us, attending community college part-time and working part-time. My daughter finally graduated with her masters and is working, also part-time, in two jobs in Massachusetts. Thank God, she is able to afford her apartment and is able to fend for herself and save some money. I would love for her to come home and save faster and own her own place rather than rent, but she prefers her independence.

If we wanted to retire, we could make some major financial decisions, like get tenants in this home and rent a smaller place for two with my husband. Or sell this home and downsize to a smaller two bedroom, two-bath home closer to his work where housing is less expensive. Yet, I have obligations or expenses still facing me: getting my son through school, rebuilding my retirement savings, which was obliterated by the last layoff during the banking and housing collapse of 2008. We have goals like funding my daughter or son's weddings in the future. Perhaps save enough to travel to various locations in the world. I also desire to leave a legacy in the form of expanding and helping to build churches as beacons of hope in this society. The choice I make about retirement, although I can taste it being unemployed right now, is to wait another ten to fifteen years. I believe I have much to offer society still and continue to be productive. I can also be wiser and disciplined about saving my hard earned money than ever before.

What is burdening my soul, and I will spill it, is that I have reconnected with various people in my past who literally worked for me at one time and are now Chief Financial Officers or Human Resource Managers and are settled in their what they feel are their secure and permanent jobs until retirement. I know to some this may be a reality, but for me I am a bit jealous that this has not transpired in my life. I look at my resume, and I have a wealth of experience but even to me, as a once hiring manager, it looks choppy. I went back to retail twice in my life as a woman in the sandwich generation, once when my son was born. He was asthmatic. I wanted to be near him in the event of an attack. Plus, I wanted a job that I could put in my 8 to 10 hours and leave and not think about it on my days off.

My second five years at Macy's, were because retail was the only one hiring after the housing and bank collapse of 2008. Plus, my father was terminally ill, in and out of emergency rooms and in hospice care. I needed to be close and available to support my mom. Now, are there women who have jobs, children, parents who have made it through the glass ceiling and are doing phenomenal work into their sixties and seventies? Yes, if you look around in various industries there are such women, even grandmothers in politics, entertainment and various industries. So I admire the women that have made it despite the odds. I am sure it took great sacrifice plus great support to achieve what they have achieved. We know Pelosi and Boxer in politics, plus Meg Whitman in technology, yet there are many others who made choices that I possibly did not make, or who had some form of mentorship or support or just the pure determination and stamina that I obviously didn't have.

In any case, these women who have made it are living proof that it can happen. You can presumably have it all marriage, family, and career. I don't know their happiness gage with each of those components of life. Some may be on their multiple marriages. Their children may or may not be a social or mental mess. I don't know about those elements in their life. The complexity of my life is that I didn't stick to it through thick and thin. I met the obstacles that came in my way, by making the choices I needed to make in support of my family. In hindsight, I would not have done anything any differently. I made the choices that were best for me in each circumstance. In my life, I made choices to uphold my family's needs first, then career, and then myself last. Perhaps, that should be inverse to some degree as me first, family second, and then career? You can spin it many ways. You have to do what is right for you in the moment at hand.

Now, that this employment has been terminated, I am contemplating my next strategic career move. With another ten to fifteen working years ahead of me, what would be the perfect thing to do? I have long envisioned writing books, being a speaker, trainer, and consultant, similar to Ken Blanchard, author of the One Minute Manager, or John Maxwell author of 21 Irrefutable Laws of Influence. Once again, I tried to find a female author, speaker, or consultant in the business realm and could not, unless there is one that is not marketed as profusely. Suzie Orman is one that comes to mind in finance, or several religious female preachers, but none specific in business.

Once again when faced with a big decision or stirring in my gut, I go to church to pray about it. I arrived early at church, and came across the young lady who leads worship songs at the church service. I told her what an amazing job she does, and I was in the service where she shared her moving story of how she turned to Jesus as her Lord and Savior. Somehow, we got talking about the decision making path that I am on right now, and I told her about potentially being on my own as an author, speaker, and consultant on faith-based approaches to business, management, and entrepreneurship. She said that sounds really good like "Ken Blanchard". I felt it was a prophetic message that she had uttered as that is the path I should take.

About a year ago, I ran across a gentleman at the post office packing a stack of books into a box for shipping. I asked him while waiting in line if he was an author. He said, "No, he is a publisher". I shared that I had written two books and working on my third, and he gave me his card to call on him. I had an appointment with him, and he said that he would market my book and me as an author for a $2500 monthly fee. I told him that amount was the value of my mortgage and not possible at this time. I know about marketing and I probably could replicate what he would intend to do: create a website, use keyword optimization to drive people to it, create e-books, audio-books, create publicity, speaking engagements. If I put my mind to it, I could probably make this happen. Have speaking engagements, trainings, to drive consulting business and sales of my books. The books legitimize you as an authority on the subjects of which you speak. The compensation is in the speaking engagements, the consulting business and some book sales. Timing becomes a critical path. I can't see this as a full time venture for me at this current time. I see it still further in my future, perhaps with more books in my authorship portfolio, or as a part-time calling. I also see it aligned with a teaching engagement at a college or university, or in a business coaching capacity.

Due to my love of continuous learning, and continuously challenging myself, I decided that I would pursue Pharmaceutical Sales. To do that I decided, not that it has an advantage or is a requirement, but rather for my own edification into this new growing industry, to obtain my Certification for National Sales Representative. I studied the material over six weeks and passed the test thinking it may eliminate a barrier to entry. Most of the job descriptions I applied for had a prerequisite of outside sales, very few were entry level, many wanted an existing market knowledge or presence to tap from. After weeks of pursuing this by on-line applications and LinkedIn, I decided to change course.

I decided that I do very well with face to face interface speaking directly with hiring managers. I thought about how I landed my previous sales job with Prudential Financial as a Financial Planner, Investment Advisor and Insurance Agent. The opportunity was presented to me at a Career Fair. I decided to search out career fairs in San Diego and Orange County, get dressed up, nails and makeup done, bring fifteen resumes, and present myself and learn about the companies actually hiring. I enjoyed it so much, talking with everyone, sharing my information. Basically, career fairs are an at the moment first interview. At the first career fair, I spoke with three companies and was successful in obtaining second interviews with two of them. At the second interview, I was very discerning about the level of satisfaction and engagement I saw from the employees, as well as the environment that the employees were expected to be productive in. This latter component was very important to me, as I want a company that lifts up their employees and creates an environment conducive to their success! That is, the management or owners care about the employees and help them to be productive.

At the second career fair, I met with two companies and landed second interviews with both companies. What was intriguing and relates back to my "Hell's Rangers" chapter in my book, The Manager From Hell, was that the hiring manager at the career fair gave me a card to call for the Human Resource Recruiter and tell her that he had given me the card to move forward with my application. When I called the Human Resource individual, as instructed, her response to me was "That's not how it's done." I was taken back a bit, and responded that "I am sorry, the manager had said to call you, and that you would forward a packet for me to complete. I was following his instructions." She said "Then he is misinformed. We gather all the resumes from the event and we review and have a discussion with the managers about them, then invite those of interest to the interview." I thanked her for her time, and said I will be patient and anticipate the process moving forward. In my mind, I wanted to say "You HR B____H! The company has spent tons of money engaging managers in an all day career fair, and the manager is excited on moving forward with a candidate, and you want to slow that down. I get that it needs to follow due process, for legal and organizational requirements. I get that. What irks me was her self-righteous dominant attitude!

How about handling the response to my call in a more customer-centric, team oriented, professional manner?   First, how about recognizing my enthusiasm in having attended a career fair this morning, met a great manager representative of your company, and eagerly followed through on the instructions given, with the hope of moving forward in obtaining a position.

Second, how about not throwing your colleague under the bus and further making the company's lack of process and hiring disorganization more glaring. How about just asking my name once again, making note of my interest and explaining the process that moves forward from that point.

In that one phone call, the human resource representative, the department that establishes the culture of the company, deflated my enthusiasm and raised my guard and discernment about the teamwork level of the company. Do I want to work in a company that doesn't know or has not properly communicated the hiring protocols? Do I want to work in a company that throws teammates under the bus? Prior to my interview, I researched the company and its social network reviews or on-line reputation. In a glassdoor.com ex-employee review, it mentioned how compensation is frequently changed to the favor of the company and the commission incentives were not clear and not in writing.

When I interviewed with the company, the environment was great, employees had smiles on their faces and made eye contact with you. I was interviewing with two managers simultaneously and in asking about the compensation, the one manager explained it one way, while the other manager corrected him and said "no, it's not calculated that way anymore". OOPS!! Can you see how this ambiguity in processes and obvious lack of communication and leadership is effecting the organization? I still came through with a scheduled interview date of one month out from the second interview. Because they are hiring a large group of individuals, the CEO and VP of Sales want to meet the individuals. My second interview was March 20th, and the third interview is scheduled for April 17th! What can we discern from this?

They must not know that the hiring market has improved, and they could lose their best candidates to other opportunities.

They must not care about individuals who are unemployed that they are stringing along for another month.

Perhaps, the CEO and VP don't trust the hiring managers at the location to make a hiring decision on their own.

Perhaps, they want to only train and hire those who absolutely want to work for them, and are willing to wait for the royal visit.

At first, I thought how great to meet the CEO and founder of the company and the VP of Sales. Perhaps, they want to ensure the quality of the organization and its representatives are upheld. Perhaps, it's just a grand-fathering gesture, showing how caring and involved management is and to welcome potential new-hires personally aboard. All I know is that 28 days of waiting is inefficient. Time is money for everyone! For me, it worked great, because the other two companies are further along on my interest scale, and I am looking for third interviews with them shortly, they said within the week from the second interview.

Through this job-hunting season of my life, there is also tax season. Plus, my transmission decides to give out on my over 10 year old vehicle, along with the water heater in our 10 year old house. Meantime, my daughter in Massachusetts says she misses mommy and thinks this is the perfect time to come visit her before I get my next job. Part of me agrees. I have frequent flyer miles for a free trip, but I also have some responsibilities to my son and husband at home. Since my unemployment, we decided to rent out my mother-in-law's room and private bath downstairs and my daughter's bedroom and bath upstairs for additional income. So, I have the coming and goings and needs of tenants to watch over. Currently, I am amidst interviews with three companies, and in the third and last interview stage of the hiring process. So leaving at this juncture and going to Massachusetts would not be the wisest decision. Preferably, I would love to be employed coming into mid-year. Average rate of finding a position is about seven months, one month for every $10,000 of earnings, assuming you have a college education.

Through this search process, I have become more cognizant of the non-college skilled trades and technical trades. Information Technology (IT) industry offers a lot of great opportunities with various software or hardware certifications, Microsoft or Cisco to name a couple. If you hone those technical skills, you can earn a great amount of money without the college degree. Technical studies in Health Sciences like various therapeutic, assistants, radiology technicians, and hands that care for the many elements of healthcare can be obtained at six month to two-year programs. There is always a need for welders, plumbers, electricians, landscapers, carpenters, and a variety of construction workers who have expertise using various equipments, trucks, tractors, and cranes! The world needs all facets of expertise to meet the needs of humanity! In the end, follow your passion, what you are good at and enjoy!

Chapter Nineteen

Live, Die or Just Exist

My daughter, at age 28, is certainly following her passion for health, proper nutrition, wellness, and fitness. She has built her career, activities, business, and friends around her core values. She is happy, fulfilled and prospering in her life. What more can a parent ask for. I am satisfied, overjoyed, and very thankful for the blessings, grace and favor the Lord has poured over my family.

Similarly, my son at now age 21 is following his dream in music, attending college, working a part-time job. Although his destination is in the future, his journey is on point. He had embraced the concept that you can achieve anything you set your mind to, as long as you act with the intent of accomplishing the goal. I have instilled, in my children, faith in themselves and the Lord above, that "They can accomplish all things through Christ who strengthens me." Also, hold true to the Word that "As a man thinks, he is."

Here is the rub. You may start with the right focus and put in the effort required and intend to complete, but life presents a fork in the journey. At that fork, one must make a decision. That decision will change and redirect the trajectory of the rest of your life. Every decision you make and I mean "EVERY" has a consequence, a result whether expected or unexpected, good, bad, or ugly. Let's break it down...when you wake up this morning, where are you? How did you get here? What and how are your surroundings? Who is or is not next to you? What you decide to do next to start each day, what thoughts you have, what emotional and physical state you are in determines the rest of your day, your interactions, and your life. Is the assessment of your surroundings, what you want or wanted out of your life? What small step can you take to change the next second or day or your life? Sometimes we don't know what to do next because we don't know our options or what is available or sound to do? What can you Google or research to be more informative about your options? What credible source can you call that will help you make a sound decision on the rest of your life? Who can you call who will listen? Who can you help to get you out of yourself and perhaps think of others who may need more than you need at this time? Can you give of your time, your talent, your touch, your hug, your story to lift up someone else and be lifted up yourself through the sharing process? Often by doing or doing for others we discover ourselves!

Let's put this in another perspective. If you read my first book, But She's Not a Guy, you know of the decision making that I had to confront as a young traditional, conservative, first born of an immigrant family, first to attend college, breaking through norms and glass ceilings in my personal and professional life. The hard part of decision making is when you intentionally choose one path in that fork; you regretfully or joyously, intentionally or unintentionally leave something, or someone behind. Sometimes, just because you decided to leave someone or something behind or to forget about it, fate has it that some things or people will follow you. You cannot always leave things behind as much as you would like. Just as importantly, not everything or everyone will follow you as you may think. It becomes really critical to build the right foundation of core values and principles, including spiritual faith, physical stamina, emotional stability, resilience and flexibility to the changes in life that sometimes hit you right between the eyes. You lose your focus for a time perhaps, have various doubts, and even don't know if you are going to make it, perhaps ready to give it all up.

My confession, admonition and love for you says: keep on fighting; don't give up; pick yourself up, dust yourself off, and try again or try something different! Forgive those who have hurt you and ask those whom you have hurt, for forgiveness. Say a prayer and keep the faith, you can and will change yourself, your surroundings, and your future to the better. Show love to those around you. Smile and reach out to others and the universe will smile back at you. Smell the roses, chase the butterflies, find shapes in the clouds, listen to the babbling brook, the running river, the breaking of the ocean waves and snap out of it: go for a run, a walk or dance! Don't just sit there moping! Get up and move and make a difference! You are important. You are needed. You are beautiful. Believe that good things and people are coming your way and evil and bad times are tied up and locked away. You are onto a new and brighter beginning! So go for it, enjoy it, receive and embrace it. Accept the favor and graciousness of God through others towards you! Be happy, be thankful, and be gracious. God loves you. I love you.

As we try to live a good life to its fullest, something may still stop us. I recently was trying to find my best friend, roommate and college sorority sister through Facebook or LinkedIn on the internet and by connecting with other old friends. None of us knew of her whereabouts or circumstances. My last connection with her was the gift she sent me for my wedding. She was then living in Greece. I went once all the way to Greece and located her retail store that she had opened in Athens, and she happened to be on an island vacation, so we missed each other. We wrote letters to each other a couple of times, but life took on its own course for each of us. Then we lost touch…

When I went back to Massachusetts on this last trip to visit my daughter who was doing her internship at Beth Israel Hospital in Brookline, I had lunch with my old school mates. At that luncheon, we all asked each other with a pit in our stomachs if anyone had heard from our friend Zoe. We are all in our mid-fifties now, and this luncheon was way overdue. Internet and cards are wonderful but having a cup of coffee or a glass of wine with someone takes the relationship to a deeper level: talking eye to eye, heart to heart, and soul to soul. Our luncheon was like time had stood still and we picked up right where we left off, catching up on our husbands (then boyfriends), our children, our parents (some sadly recently passed), careers, and our own selves. Let's just say we flooded the place with laughter, tears and intense heartfelt emotions. We all felt that something was wrong with Zoe. About a week later, having returned to California, someone who had stayed in touch with the family, posted that she had passed and the funeral was soon. My soul was settled that two of my friends were able to attend the funeral in Connecticut. I am grateful to the Lord that I was able to have lunch with my other three college roommates and dear life-friends, and that we in solidarity had remembered Zoe. Perhaps in spirit she was at the table with us. Had I known she was ill, I would have been at her bedside!! We heard that she had struggled with leukemia.

More recently, after having been in Massachusetts and looking up my best friends in High School and college, I found out that one of my high school friends had moved to San Diego near me with her job. Quickly, I started looking for her and trying to get together. We finally did get together and I asked her how long had she been in California so I know where my anger meter should read? She said five years, but it was a hard and long five years. She is a corporate marketing and sales director for a medical device company, and travels extensively with work. She married off her oldest son recently and was wrapped up in those plans. Her husband struggled with health and had a triple bypass. In the last three years, she was fighting breast cancer with chemo treatments and was a twice survivor and currently in remission and hoping to remain in good health. My anger meter, turned quickly to my sad and then happy meter! Happy that I did not lose this dear friend to cancer! Five years ago, I had lost a dear neighbor, who was my son's best friend's mom, to cancer. Losing friends and loved ones is the hardest part of growing up and the hardest cycle of life to endure. All one can say is that in the Lord's measure of time, they had completed their divine purpose on earth, and their heavenly purpose in the next life is about to start. Being a Christian, I do believe in the afterlife and that death is a departure from this world to another world in heaven. One day the mystery will unfold, and I do believe I will see those who passed family and friends again in the afterlife where they are in peace, no pain, no chemo, and no meds.

So where does all this talk in this chapter bring us? Life is not a dress rehearsal. Young people have coined the phrase or abbreviation YOLO which stands for You Only Live Once. Some have interpreted that phrase inwardly so they are running marathons, climbing mountains, skydiving, scuba diving, etc. I would like to take a more extrovert approach as to what positive impact can I have today on society at large and let's start with those whom I interact with today. Be good to yourself, but don't stop there, think of what simple acts of kindness you can do for others. That little self-sacrifice will be a hundred fold rewards back to you. You will be surprised at how you reap what you sow, and how great and intense that harvest will be!

You may say what I do doesn't matter. Everything and everyone matters! We are in this world together and our interactions, our efforts and our speech is what makes this world go around. Your smile may encourage someone today and smiles are infectious. I was visiting my daughter in New York one time, and then my uncle in Boston. Being from California and having the positive, optimistic nature and outlook that I have, I naturally smile all the time. I also say hi to passersby on occasion. Both my daughter and my uncle told me that people may think you are crazy if you smile too much on the subway or on the streets of NYC or downtown Boston. Saying hello to people you don't know is not acceptable everywhere. They may lash out at you, because they are angry or mad. Wow! I looked at my California beach raised daughter on the train sitting at a seat across me and she had that train grimace down well. I smiled at her purposefully and she laughed as she couldn't hold it in. We laughed at the world and how people had to have their serious "don't mess with me face" on during their commutes in the city. Those who walk and talk on their cell phones announcing "I am busy, I am important" face on. Or those with their Starbuck coffee cup on the go all the time…you just wonder what they could have done with the opportunity cost of their latte money!! I say to all of them in our California valley girl talk "whateverrrr".

The one thing I have learned in life is not to be luke warm. The bible talks about this as well. Some people live life with indifference. Everything is maybe or gray or tolerable in their life. The world doesn't improve or move forward if that is the case. There is a story about Einstein, and I don't know if it is a true story, but it is applicable in making this point. Einstein did not speak until age five, and his parents were concerned. One day he was having soup and he suddenly spoke and said "Soup is hot". The parents were perplexed and happy and said, "Why haven't you spoken until now?" He said everything was perfect until now. If you want to accept the status quo then enjoy it and remain silent, but if you don't like something it is important in order to change it for the better to speak up, take action, write a letter, make a phone call, set up a meeting, go out and vote, etc.. Do positive things to improve the circumstances of your life and hopefully others' lives. The point is don't just exist and give up and not try. Roll up your sleeves and do it yourself, ask others to help you, start a business, employ others, don't wait on the government or your parents or others to do for you unless you have a real disability. If you have a disability, ask yourself what am I ABLE to do and do it. Be an encouragement to others and do for yourself whatever you are ABLE to do. Live life to the fullest possible, with respect and love for others and this universe.

Chapter Twenty

Ninety Minus Thirty Is Sixty

When my husband visits his mother at the old age home, she introduces him as "my little one." Her little one is now sixty years old and her oldest is 67. Yet her anticipation is that they have the same level of energy and time as her sons when they were thirty or newlyweds. Everything pivots from the day they were married, and had a wife then children, but in her mind they are still her little boys and need to drive 100 miles to visit her more often.

My mother-in-laws father passed when she was about age thirty. He died young. Her mother died when my husband was about eight years old. That would have put my mother in law about mid-forties. Similarly, my mom lost her mother when her mother was age 62, so my mom was early forties. My grandfather outlived his wife about three years and died at age 75.

With the sandwich generation, we have parents living to age ninety. My husband's mother is age 94. He has an aunt by marriage, no blood line, his father's brother's wife who had no children and is age 98. My mother gave birth to me when she was 21 and she is now age 78 and doing well. All three are on cholesterol and blood pressure medication, plus my mom takes medication for late onset diabetes.   However, these elders are fairly demanding. When they ask you to help them with something, they expect immediacy in the response time.

We always have a to-do list. Fix the TV, the computer or a lock. Replace the light bulb, or take out the trash. Explain the extra charge on the cable or telephone or any bill, and also explain why it's different from the past months. Explain the bank statements and what to do with CDs that may be coming to maturity. Take them to the eye doctor, dentist, physical therapist, nutritionist, orthopedic doctor, foot doctor, and other specialists. Go to several stores to get specific groceries on sale at various locations, regardless of the gas or time being spent. The demands are many, and no one understands that you are old as well.

When you start getting over fifty-five and you are still working full-time and caring about your college age or now graduated children, the balancing act continues. Now you are trying to help your young adults with the most important decisions of their life, a career and a companion. From all the layoffs that our generation has endured, mine going on three perhaps four; whatever you want to call them Reductions in force, golden parachutes, early voluntary retirement incentives, terminations for sundry reasons they concocted, you know that career could be a five year decision. Unless you have invested hundreds of thousands of dollars towards a life dedication like a doctor, careers are not as committed as a companion. Some readers may differ; yet, I do believe that the life companion decision is such a huge lifetime commitment. If you are going into the marriage with the concept that if doesn't work out there is always divorce, then don't get married at all.

If you later decide to have children, with the concept that "oh, I will let a nanny or grandma raise the child;" then, don't have the children, unless you plan to dedicate your life to raising your own child. If you let others raise your child, don't be surprised if you don't understand them later, or they do things that you may not do or agree with, or if they don't seem interested in you at all. Marriage and parenthood are a solemn life commitment and should not be entered into lightly as they require work and sacrifice; in return, there is immense joy and love!

So here I am age 57 and my husband age 60, with my son age 21 at home and going to college. My mom, age 78, thinks that since the interest rates are at zero percent at this time and Social Security is not providing the CPI increase at this time, it may be smart if she rents out her house and moves in with me. All is good. I love my mother. But I still have the desire for my husband. I want to entertain friends and don't necessarily want to have my mother at each gathering. My husband needs his freedom as well, and he may want to walk around with his underpants on. The whole thing is very frustrating! What if I want to retire and sell my house, then what happens? Once we are together in the same home, are we then inseparable? My distant cousin said to me, since her mother recently passed, "I wish my mom could come and live with me!" It's all relative I suppose.

The future is unknown. What type of elderly people will we be? I am trying very hard to stay healthy and active. Thank God that my husband and I are in good health and neither on any medication. No one knows what the future holds so today is all we have and I want to live it fully with my husband as much as I can.

I noticed that my parents were workaholics as a requirement of and a means of survival as immigrants in a new country. Both worked long hours to make ends meet and to provide for us. We were very appreciative of their sacrifice and we were good children, latchkey kids, good neighborhoods and good neighbors that kept watch over each other's children. So my mother because she moved to a new country, then from the east coast to the west coast, did not gather any friends and the few she has are not nearby. To her, life is all about family. Her children and grandchildren are her life. The people in her life outside of her family, particularly now that she is retired, you can count on one hand. So we are her entertainment. Thank God for our 98 years young aunt and my sister's mother in law, and Facebook. Wiith Facebook, my mother has found her old friends from Jerusalem and Massachusetts, her cousins and other family in Canada and United States.

So I told my husband, this is our challenge also, to maintain old friends and yet gather new ones. Finding time for friends seems hard, we are not used to it. Every gathering at our home as we were growing up was with family, cousins, aunts, grandparents. So we are learning to be hospitable and inclusive of others. Believe it or not, we are learning from our own adult children that seem to balance work, play and travel so much better than us. It's especially healthy when you see other members of the sandwich generation going through the same complexities and you help each other with suggestions about child rearing, adolescence, young adults, colleges, careers, various vices alcohol, drugs, sex, and eldercare, health and wellness and how to maintain your sanity through it all. There is comfort in misery!

So we repeatedly are telling our 70 to 100 year old elders, that we are not the young teenagers that their minds still consider us. That our strength and time is waning also and we plan to live our life and what is left of it together. We try to include them as much as we can in our life events, and have gatherings where they are with us, but it can't be every event every weekend. We cannot be their constant entertainment! This is easier said than done. I keep holding on to the biblical phrase "You reap what you sow". So our conviction is to care for our elders and hope that our children notice our tenderness towards them, and will remember to treat us likewise with kindness – passing it forward.

It's interesting how parents forget that we are older. Consider though that their parents passed away at a much earlier age. Both our parents didn't have parents when they were in their sixties. Yet as parents they feel the urge to tell us even when we are sixty whether we are dressed appropriately, or who we should or not invite to an event, what we should buy or not buy, it's frustrating. It's an urge that we in the sandwich generation must inspect in ourselves as well as our millennial children are staying home longer, taking their sweet time to graduate, waiting on the economy to improve to land their ideal desired career job, and postponing out of financial necessity or fear of commitment to form households. How often have I heard from my children, "Stop telling me what to do!" or "I know that already?" Of course, they know it. They are so resourceful with Google at their fingertips. Knowledge is rampant!

I had written a poem when I was in my late teens, that I found as I was perusing my files and keepsakes, which reflects what my children are saying to me now as they try to launch their life. It also is relevant in my late fifties, as I explain to my mother that I am not a child, I am a woman with a husband, children, career and a life to live! Here is the poem called "Let Me Breath."

Let Me Breath

I can no longer stand the pain
Of someone pulling at my reins.
I can no longer endure
The grip of love.

Don't hold on to me
Let me fall.
I'd like to find out if I can walk alone
Or still need to crawl.

Let me go.
Let me experience.
If you expect danger always
I'll miss the wonder and excitement.

I know you love me
But please let me breath.
My mistakes will be mine
And I'm sure I will be fine.

Let me decide
What's right for me
Let me breath
And free to just be.

Chapter Twenty-one

Tempering Expectations

I am coming to the realization that everyone needs to temper their expectations. The more you expect from others, the more disappointed you will be. Expecting from others is a sure road to dissolution and depression. Replace your expectations of everyone else to do things for you, to your liking and to your timing, with zero expectations of them. Instead, turn the table around to yourself and ask, "what can I do today to give myself and others joy?" It could be simple tasks like organize the kitchen pantry or hallway closet, or color coordinate the wardrobe in your closet. It can be writing a letter to a friend, or picking up the phone and calling someone to see how they are doing and what is new in their life. Take a walk around the block of your own neighborhood and say hello to neighbors that may be outside gardening or playing ball with their children or walking their dogs.

As we age the tables, the schedules, the busy times have turned around. At one time, we were running around with our children to the ballet classes, the soccer games, and the recitals. Now, they are grown and independent adults just like we wanted, driving themselves to work or school or out with friends. We and the grandparents have to understand that they may not need us always and in every circumstance, and we all have to let go. Having taken the time to provide the values, the discernment, the understandings and precautions when they were young, we have to have faith and trust them and the Lord above and His guardian angels to let our children free-to-be in this world to make choices for themselves. Now we just need to be there, when they need us. This is easier said than done!

Here also is a layer of generational confrontation. We have our parents judging our parental skills and decisions! "How can you let them….?" Or

"When are they going to…?" Sometimes in the sandwich generation we have to deal with questions after repeated question from our own parents, bombarding us and second guessing your parental decisions. They often forget that we raised our children and we are their parents and times have changed. Now, we too have to understand, and often forget, that our parents went through changing times as well. It's all right for everyone to hear each other out and to determine cohesively as to the best approach in a given situation. Sometimes, it does take a village depending on the importance or severity of a situation. We have to understand one another and know that some words and actions come from a place of love. We all have to also check ourselves to not be overly critical, demanding, or harsh with our words or actions. The unfortunate loving truth is sometimes we have to allow others to fail to learn from mistakes, however much we want to shelter them from the mistakes we made. We also have to remember that our mistakes were under different circumstances, environments, and times. What may have failed us in our day could, very well be, a tremendous success for them in their time and moment in life. We have to be flexible and open minded in many ways and respect each other's opinions. At times, we also need to agree to disagree, and choose peace over being right.

Remember when your children were little and they wanted something and they wanted it NOW! As a member of the sandwich generation, I am finding elders are just as impatient. They want their handyman jobs to be done now. The light bulb changed, the bank called, the ride to pick up a sale item, fixing the computer for the multitude time, all done yesterday! They must know their time is short, so they want everything done today, often at the most inopportune moment for you, as it always works out. So here is when we all have to flex our patience muscles! Sandwich generation has to prioritize who and what is important and be able to communicate that to others in a succinct and polite way. We have to learn to schedule everything and know how to manage others expectation of us. Most importantly, we have to not expect too much of ourselves or we will disappoint ourselves. Take on what we can take on, and communicate to others what will have to wait and why. Clearly define it, no time, no money, no expertise, no time to schedule or make the appointment, other priorities have to be met first…spell it out! Also, delegate back some things…can you call your sister, your best friend, your neighbor, your other daughter-in-law. Perhaps you can split the task, so if you do this part, I can do this part and have it done at this time…Also, provide alternatives…what if you do this instead in the meantime…maybe this will work better even… We all have to be open and not so myopic in what needs to be done and when. Often, we are our own worst enemy and our expectations of ourselves can drain our minds and bodies. Take a breath, relax, its ok!

Chapter Twenty-two

Centennial Celebration

Auntie Ann is now coming into her one hundredth birthday. She says to me that she wants to have a birthday party and celebration. She wants to take everyone out to dinner. She has prepared a list of forty guests that she plans to invite. She is truly remarkable to be so engaged and enthusiastic about life and living! She said we have to have favors for the party and had her caretaker take her out to shop for a special item that will be a memoir for the guests. She found these huge mugs with a colorful array of candles all surround and asked my opinion and I said they were perfect, as they were!

She has such heart and soul at one hundred. She always says "Don't worry about anything honey. Things always resolve themselves. It all works out in the end as it is intended." Truly, it all doesn't matter. I have come to the realization what really matters in life is being true to yourself, working or doing what you enjoy, keeping life simple and elegant, being around or with people that matter to you whom you have a mutual respect and love, and care for each other and who walk in truth with you. That is, real and unconditional, not hypocritical, judgmental or pretentious. Be with the people who you can trust, and who trust you and you can be together in both happiness and sadness. You don't always have to agree, but you can talk and share opinions truthfully with each other. Various trusting or trustworthy people can provide you with constructive advice, caution, and ideas. Always remember your source and their experience or background. You can always listen to advice given out of love, but you can weigh it, use it, and store it in the recesses of your mind to apply later, or throw it away. Receiving information from a credible source and measuring your response and action to that information are in your hands. Some people out of love share something they have experienced, which is not relevant in your life or could even be factually untrue. You are not required to accept everything you hear as a truth regardless of who in authority is sending it your way…not a parent, or teacher, or friend, or enemy. Remember to understand the reference point and understand the source, their background and experience, and accept what you feel deems correct, truthful and applicable to your life and circumstances. In the same light, do not throw away salient, loving advice, because it may be painful to hear. The truth may hurt in the short term, but often sets you free in the long term.

There is an old adage about "don't throw away the baby with the dirty bath water." This is where your own critical thinking and due diligence comes in. For example, if you have something in your life, a vice, or something or someone who your whole family advises you is toxic to your health or wellbeing, you can't just throw the family and their advice out. Give yourself the time and the due respect to yourself and family and friends who are probably looking out for your best interest to assess the situation and the circumstance and come to a reasonable conclusion.   You have to give the time to assess where and what the truth of the matter is and its relevance, and then take the steps necessary based on the truth that you have discerned in a fully conscious manner.

There are those times when you have to follow your gut or your heart or your mind or some fusion of the three. The debate between those three factions can be gut wrenching, heart breaking and mind boggling! It certainly is a battle that takes intense resolve to win and decipher. Prayer, meditation, communication, exercise, sleep may all be needed to come to a determination. That is why it is so important to know thyself and stay true to your values in life, in work, in love and in play. When you work against the grain of your own core values, principles and likes, your whole body, soul and mind are thrown for a tailspin. Sometimes this whirlwind is unrecognizable, and the longer it lasts, the deeper the lies to yourself, it becomes harder and harder to see the light of day at the end of the tunnel. It's where depression, disease, anxiety all settle into the nest that has been prepared for such demons that are fed by disillusionment, more lies leading to more unhappiness; hence, the spiral. Living a fake life, not aligned with your own values, can make you physically and emotionally ill.

So how does one last one hundred years, still smile and be full of life and energy and desire to go on to have a centennial celebration?

Blended

After many years,

We are truly blended.

We laugh together,

And smile at each other,

Even finish each other's sentences.

Our thoughts are one thought.

Our bodies are one body.

Our values and goals are alike.

Through trials and testing,

Through tears and laughter,

Ours souls have merged

And our hearts are blended.

Chapter Twenty-three

The Desire to Live

At 4:33 am on one Friday morning, I woke up with a revelation. So strong was this revelation that came to me in the early dawn that I had to sit up and write it down on my trusty notebook that waits expectantly on my nightstand. My pen takes a life of its own as my hand starts writing feverishly while thoughts are pouring from my head down my hand and through my fingers!

God is a God of patterns! He teaches us through parables, nature and animals as to how to live our lives. The birds do not worry rather they flutter and go about their business. The eagles that sore above the wind, they don't let the wind take them off their course, they use the wind to surge higher! The ants that work hard, carrying more than their own weight at times, just stay on the job of storing their food prior to the rains. The gazelles that run for their lives from their predators, they understand the ominous food chain!

What was revealed to me is that God is a God of order, patterns, in the real sense a mathematician. The minutes, the hours, the days, the seasons, the rotation of the earth, the moon and the tides, all is in a divine pattern that cannot be undone or controlled, although humans have attempted to understand and manipulate it. The complexity is too grand for us humans to cohesively and completely understand. God loves multiplication! Often promising his believers double, tenfold, seven fold, hundred fold for living in the path God has offered them, a narrow and simple path of goodness, with love and kindness towards all, and that includes towards our self.

Consider also the speed of light, and the speed by which the days fall into the night and life passes by. Contemplate on Einstein's experiments to try to understand the speed of light and time travel theories. I recently began locating old friends and classmates through the internet and social media and discovered that with friends of the heart; you can pick up the conversation exactly where you left off, like it was only yesterday, as though time didn't really exist and you didn't miss a beat.

Then I thought about helixes and the universe and how the sun is the center and the planets spin in a specific orbit around that sun. They need to remain in the orbit with a specific distance from the sun so they don't get lost or fall out of orbit, so they don't get burned or dematerialize. They stay in orbit revolving around the sun. I akin that to humans staying close to God and going about our business in a specific order by hanging on to God's words and in continuous communication with him in all matters large or small in our lives. Our source of strength, provision, protection, wisdom, understanding, peace, love and happiness is in direct relation with our daily walk with God as we go about our lives. The further away we get from our specified orbit, and our life source, the more lost, depressed, frustrated, defeated, and victimized we feel.

Here is a theory: Time perhaps is like DNA strands twisted together and then also orbiting around the son, God or Jesus Christ. Perhaps we are traveling on those strands and also orbiting. To maintain ourselves in orbit, God needs to be our source of energy; our daily bread is His word. In this way, we will feel fulfilled and everything will feel like it is in place, in order and well with us. This is also a generational issue. A lost parent, one who does not know God or his own divine purpose takes matters in their own hands, shuns God by turning to vices (porn, drugs, alcohol, abuse, infidelity, crime, etc); their offspring also become lost and must search even harder to find Jesus for themselves in order to gain order in their life. So many phrases come to mind like "what goes around comes around" or "you reap what you sow" or "the circle of life". My revelation suggests that we are not in a time line with a beginning and an end, but rather a twisted strand or an orbit, a continuum, where you may be getting closer in time as you age back to where you started. Your body is older, but you do not feel older. When you live in love and peace, relationships feel the same at 60 as they did when you were twenty as though time has stood still. When you look at a child now 21 and reflect on when she or he was one as though it was only yesterday. Perhaps it was only yesterday. Déjà vu…you have been there before…as you orbit through time…

We are not just experiencing time passing away, but our personal orbit around God, and the people that we hold dear are on path also on these helixes or strands of their own individual lives like chromosomes, genes, electrons, protons and neutrons. We are members of God's body. He is the nucleus, the center and we are energized by him to do specific jobs and purposes that He defined in our genes and DNA for us to accomplish. By staying in orbit, and revolving around God, we can understand the fullness of how our life is to play out. I do believe in heaven and hell. Staying on track and following God's guidance spelled out in a time tested true book the Bible or Breath of God, which is God's promise to us, His covenant with us for a fruitful and happy life. One of God's promises to us, and the essence of the Gospel is in John 3:16 "For God so loved the world, that He gave his only begotten son, so whomsoever believes in Him, shall not perish and shall have everlasting life." The inverse of that are those who don't believe and are not committed to God's word will perish and not have everlasting life. Those who are lost, spinning out of orbit, away from God are perishing now as we speak, they are floating around like burning space junk, zombies, the walking dead, as they have no energy or life within them.

The beauty of God's promise is all they have to do is believe in Jesus and ask Him to come into their life and show them the path that He wants them to follow. It is so simple, so easy, so narrow and He awaits them with open arms…all they need to do is ask that Jesus come into their lives and as Carrie Underwood's song says "Jesus, take the wheel" and see how God creates new glorious paths for them. It will undeniably be God, as He wants to be known to you and be in your life. He is not an imposing God. He leaves the choice up to you. It is his gift of grace, there is no test to pass,…"whomsoever" not just perfect people…"whomsoever" includes all of us, anyone,…it includes "you"… Just ask Jesus to be in your life, renew your spirit, and to show you the way! He forgives and forgets and erases completely your past, and starts you a new! With Jesus in your life, you can be happy at any age, even beyond 100, and you can live forever with your loved ones in our next home called heaven.

After the final publication of this book, my aunt is now 102 and still celebrating life! God bless her and my mother, now 82, the two inspirational women currently in my life. I am truly blessed to have them to talk with and often lean on for wisdom and guidance.

ABOUT THE AUTHOR

Ms. Hasmik Rakijian, born in Kuwait, and raised in Massachusetts, has worked in Michigan and California, with special assignments in Wisconsin, Pennsylvania, and Minnesota. She studied accounting at Bentley University in Waltham, MA and obtained her Bachelors in Business Administration Finance from San Diego State University and a Masters of Arts in Organizational Management from University of Phoenix. She also holds a certificate in Lean Six Sigma from Villanova University. She has had escalating responsibility in corporate accounting and financial management to the level of Corporate Controller in industries as computer hardware and software manufacturing and development, semiconductors, peripherals and steel fabrication, construction. She also has had significant inside and outside sales experience in a variety of industries as retail, cosmetics, precious metals, weight loss, financial planning, investments and insurance. Regardless of the career sacrifices she has had to make for childcare or eldercare issues in her life, as evidenced by her "zigzag" or "yo-yo" resume, she has learned to be resilient, open to learn new things and continues to reinvent, change and grow! Trying to be a supportive wife, a good mother, daughter, niece, sister and sister-in-law is exhausting to say the least. Thus emergence of this book regarding her experiences in the sandwich generation, and how she tries to keep the endorphins coming to keep her sanity and stay happy while meeting her commitments! Realize that understanding relationships through time, accepting generational similarities and differences, and doing frequent self-assessments in order to live life to the fullest takes effort, inclusion and love.